Settling in Spain

Our new life between the mountains and the sea

Doreen B. Tonks

ISBN-13: 978-1500979447

ISBN-10: 1500979449

For my husband Ken,
whose patience and long absences
have made the writing of this book possible.

1

It just came to me one day while I was defrosting the sprouts for Sunday dinner. Ken's mother always insists on sprouts, although once a year at Christmas is enough for me, and for some reason it was then that I thought about that programme we'd just seen about all those people being conned out of their savings in Spain. We could do that, I thought – not lose our savings, of course, but move to Spain. So while I sat there watching Ethel, that's Ken's mum, picking bits of sprout off her dentures I thought that one really good thing about living in Spain would be not having to watch her do that every other week.

It might not sound like enough of a reason to emigrate, and it might not be a very nice thing to say, but after I'd started reading my way through all the books about people who have gone to live in Spain I decided to start writing things down in case *I* wanted to write a book about it later on. Those writers are always truthful about their experiences so I think I should be too, sprouts and all.

When Ken's mother had finally gone I waited for the motor racing to finish before I sat down opposite him and broached the subject.

"Where was the Grand Prix today, Ken?" I asked.

"Monza."

"Oh, is that in Spain?"

"Italy."

"We could move to Spain, you know, when you retire next year."

"What?" he said, before getting up to put the kettle on, but I could see that I had planted a seed.

I'll always remember that first conversation we had and in the weeks to come we had many more. I started leaving some of the books that I'd read on his bedside table – the ones where things go well right from the start, not the ones where everything is a disaster before it all comes out all right in the end – and I'm sure that he looked at them because I could see that they had moved from one day to the next. He wasn't at all enthusiastic at first because he's never been overkeen on foreigners, but every day I told him something new about how good it was living in Spain – how cheap it is, how nice the weather is (though he knew that already), how happy they are to have British people buying their houses, and how few foreigners live there, except the Spanish, and little by little he began to see the light.

It was one Wednesday evening late in November when we had another memorable conversation that I will always remember. The English wind was howling outside and Ken put down his pipe and cleared his throat.

"It'd have to be near the coast, Doreen," he said, just like that.

"Yes, dear," I said, trembling a little but trying not to show it.

"With plenty of other Brits around so we'd have someone to talk to."

"Yes, dear," I said, my heart beating faster.

"Bob says he and Maureen might start looking at places in some town near Benidorm."

"Yes, dear," I said again, speechless. I can't abide Bob's wife Maureen – she has a tattoo on her wrist – but I didn't show it. I knew that he trusted his friend Bob with his life, despite him being a traffic warden, and I waited with bated breath for him to speak.

"We could have a week out there in the spring. Rent a car and have a look around."

"YES, dear," I almost shouted, before putting down my tray and rushing over to hug him.

"Get off," he said, but nicely, "I'm off down the pub."

You cannot imagine how long that winter was, waiting for spring to come around. Nothing but rubbish on TV night after night, but I read through most of it – even Emmerdale – and by March I think I'd read just about every word ever printed about living in Spain, even one book that was written over thirty years ago when hardly anybody lived there. After all that reading I felt like I was living there already which, considering that it had been eight years since we'd had our last fortnight there – in Lanzarote, an island, but still belonging to Spain – just shows how good some of the books were. They made Spanish people seem so jolly and even a bit eccentric, in a nice way, and not at all like some of the miserable waiters and hotel staff we'd come across on our travels over the years. Ken said that they've probably cheered up after seeing how many of us go over there to keep their miserable economy afloat, which was just one of his little jokes.

As the date for our flight to Malaga approached my sense of trepidation reached fever pitch. Would I like it? Would I really want to live there? Would it be as good as it was in most of the books? Ken said it was just a blinking week and that I needn't have packed ten days beforehand, but nothing could quell my desire to set foot on Spanish soil. Ken had said why didn't we take a peek at the place where Bob and Maureen might be going to live, but I said that the weather was much nicer right down in the south and that we'd be near Gibraltar in case we got homesick. I *didn't* say it was because that woman wouldn't be there, as he's so close to Bob despite his vulgar wife.

We caught the plane at Manchester and it is at this point that I must say that I have decided to change the names of all the places in the book, except Manchester and Malaga. This is because in most of the best books that I've read about Spain this is what they tend to do. I think it's because if the book sells like hotcakes they'll not want people coming to nose around. Bob says it's probably because what they write is a pack of lies, but that's just Bob's way. We come from a town not too far from Manchester and where we have come to live you will soon see, but I'm getting ahead of myself.

When we stepped off the plane that morning at Malaga Airport and my sandalled foot touched the tarmac I became quite emotional. Ken became emotional too because it was chucking it down and our feet were getting soaked. I told him that the weather wasn't always like this and he said that he bloody well knew that, but to get a move on to the terminal building. I don't like Ken swearing but if the book if to be as honest as the others are I feel that I have to report what he says as he says it and not 'tone it down' as I'm sure they do in some of the less truthful books.

That week in Spain was an adventurous step for us as there was no tour guide and coach to meet us like on our previous holidays and we knew we would have to fend for ourselves. When we finally found the car rental place and left the airport, Ken cursing each time he banged his hand into the door in search of the gearstick, it was an exciting moment. What would become of us? Where would we end up? Ken pulled over on the airport road and after some more cursing got the tom-tom to work and after a short drive on the motorway we found our way to the hotel we had booked in Fuentecastillo, half an hour to the right of Malaga city. (That's not its real name but I've named two real places already and that's quite enough, Ken says.)

After we were shown to our room by a surly young man it felt like the adventure had really begun. Where would we have dinner? What would we eat? What would we do with ourselves until we met the estate agent at eleven the following morning? In the end we had lamb chops in the hotel restaurant – Ken cursing the measly chops, soggy chips, the rude waitress and the price – before walking down to the front for an evening stroll. The sky had cleared, although by then it was dark, and our sandals were almost dry as we pattered along the promenade and talked of our future life in Spain.

"How do you feel now, Ken?" I asked.

"Them greasy chips haven't agreed with me," he replied.

"Yes, but I mean about us being out here."

"At least it's stopped raining."

"Are you looking forward to tomorrow?" I asked.

"Hmm, I don't trust estate agents," he replied, glowering at the moon.

"Well at least he's English."

"Yes, I wouldn't touch a Spanish one. I wouldn't trust them an inch."

"But we don't really know the Spanish yet, Ken. In the books most of them are nice, loyal, amusing and things."

"Ah, in the books they might be," he said mysteriously, before stopping to light his pipe.

Ken always speaks in that half grumpy half wise way of his, but as the story unfolds you will see that deep down he has a heart of gold much of the time.

"Let's get back," he said, between puffs of his pipe. "My feet are bloody freezing."

The next morning I arose at eight and rushed to pull up the blind to let the sunshine come streaming into our hotel room, before lowering it again after a low moaning sound and a pillow reached me from the bed. We breakfasted at ten (no Full English on the menu, much to Ken's disgust) before waiting on the patio for the estate agent. He arrived five minutes early with a cheery good morning and introduced himself as Malcolm, which I already knew after speaking to him on the phone.

Malcolm was in his early thirties, about five feet eleven, slim apart from a small beer belly, and was wearing brown shoes, beige casual trousers, a red and brown checked shirt and a big gold looking watch. His light hair was cut short and his slightly bloodshot blue eyes beamed at us from his smooth, tanned face.

"Hello folks," he said. "I'm Malcolm."

Ken's brow clouded when he realised that he was a southerner and when Malcolm went to fetch the car I made haste to assure my husband that the testimonials on his computer website proved that he was a trustworthy man.

"At least he's not Spanish," Ken said, somewhat soothed. "Let's see what he's got to show us."

First Malcolm drove us along the coast – to the right or the left I shall not say – to see an apartment with a narrow sea view between other apartment blocks. As we went up in the lift to the fourth floor Malcolm explained that he wanted to show us a good selection of what was on offer in our price range and that *under no circumstances* did he want us to rush into a decision. He said he felt responsible for our future happiness, which made up for his breath smelling slightly of alcohol probably caused by a wonderful Spanish night out the like of which can only be had in Spain.

The apartment was spacious and newish with nice narrow balconies and without any carpets, of course, as they don't use them in Spain. I quite liked it, but when Malcolm asked us what we thought Ken said that he wouldn't live in a flat over his own dead body, which made enough sense for Malcolm to lead us back down to the car. He then said that he quite understood that people of our class would prefer to live in a house but that unfortunately it was difficult to find a house in our price range right near the coast unless we wanted a terraced one. Ken's ironic grunt told him that we didn't, so he drove up a road which went under the motorway and soon we were climbing past tree-laden fields into the hills.

After about twenty minutes and a lot of serpentine bends we reached a mostly white village where Malcolm parked before taking us to see a three-storey house at the end of a narrow street. Anticipating Ken's grunts or comments he said that although it was technically terraced it was the end house and did have a spacious garden in need of a little 'TLC'. After I had explained to Ken what 'TLC' meant we walked through the old house into a medium-sized rubbish dump. Malcolm said that all the prams, pallets and other debris would be removed before the sale and he began to wax lyrical about the perfect situation of the house – not far from the sea but with the advantage of the pure mountain air and the friendly comings and goings of the villagers.

When Ken asked if there were many other British people living there Malcolm paused for a moment as if trying to weigh up which would be the best answer to give. I think he thought that Ken's constant grunting meant that he was an unsociable soul so he said that no, there were very few other foreigners in the village and that it was a great place for peace and quiet. A minute later we were back on the road heading further up the mountain and after many more dizzying bends and a long time spent behind a stubborn tractor driver we came to a larger, whiter village against a backdrop of stunning mountains which took my breath away. I think Ken was impressed too because the moment he got out of the car he lit his pipe – often a sign of strong emotions in my husband.

Malcolm parked in a small square and led us through some very quaint and narrow streets to a modern two-storey house on the edge of the village. This one had a proper, though not overlarge, garden and commanded fine views from the bedroom windows. Malcolm said that the beauty of the place was that although it preserved its traditional village life there were also quite a number of British people living there which meant that there were several bars and restaurants where one could meet ones compatriots and have a chinwag. When Ken asked him if there were foreigners from other countries there Malcolm had another of his pensive pauses before saying that no, there weren't very many and that the very few that there were were mostly Scandinavians who spoke good English. Malcolm interpreted Ken's slight nod as a positive sign and went on extolling the virtues of the house and the village until Ken left us and went to explore the other rooms.

On the drive back down to the coast my husband was eerily silent and even Malcolm practically stopped talking, seemingly resigned to not having pleased him with his selection of properties. When he stopped to drop us off outside the hotel Ken grunted a brief goodbye and went inside, leaving me to thank him for showing us the houses and asking for his card. My heart was heavy as I trudged into the bar where I found Ken ordering a beer and I waited until we were seated – Ken with his beer and me with a café con leche (coffee with milk) – before I asked him what he thought of our day's exploration with Malcolm.

"I'm not buying anything off that bloody ponce," he said firmly.

"No, dear," I replied.

"And I'm not living in a flat or anywhere where no-one speaks English," he went on.

"No, dear."

"But that second village was all right and if there are plenty of other Brits living there it'd be a nice place to live. We'll not buy yet though. We could rent first of all to see if we like it."

Struck dumb by his torrent of words I nodded enthusiastically and grasped his left arm ardently.

"You'll spill my beer, you daft cow," he said with a fleeting smile on his face.

The next day we got in our hire car, switched on the tom-tom, and headed back to the village which had so captivated my husband and myself. There seemed to be even more bends than the day before but I felt safe beside Ken as he manoeuvred the vehicle skilfully onwards and upwards. He pointed out that we'd have to make sure there was a decent supermarket and that it sold some English food as he was damned if he'd be traipsing down to the coast every week to do the shopping.

In the course of the coolly overcast day we found that there were two small supermarkets and that one of them sold Branston Pickle, Weetabix, Ovaltine and other basic foodstuffs. We also ascertained that there were indeed many other English-looking people sitting around on the café terraces, all looking very brown or red and mostly happy to be there. My only nervous moment came when we were having lunch – a paella which the waiter told us was a speciality of the village – and Ken swore that the two couples sitting at the next table were speaking German. After they had gone Ken asked the waiter where they were from and it was a great relief to me when the young man said they were 'Holland people'.

Over coffee (con leche) I suggested to Ken that we stop by the English estate agency which we had spotted to ask about house rentals, which we did. Lo and behold, they were southerners too and of the sort that especially annoy my husband with their whiny voices and false laughter (Ken said) but they did give us an idea of the prices and we went away with a card. After we had stepped outside, Ken's energetic puffing on his pipe told me that he was coming up with an idea and I waited silently while he formulated it. He finally said that we should nip back to the restaurant where we had had dinner (meaning lunch) because he wanted a word with that waiter.

Shrouded in mystery, I followed him in and soon all was revealed. Ken asked the waiter if he knew anybody who could translate for us in our quest for a house to rent and the waiter, Juan by name, said that he himself would be happy to carry out this task if we could return the following day, his day off, and that, yes, he knew of properties to rent.

"No flats," said Ken.

"No flats," repeated Juan.

"How much for the day?" asked Ken.

"Fifty euros," answered Juan, and hands were shaken all round.

On the even more sinuous seeming drive back down to the coast I remarked to Ken that I was surprised that he had hired the services of a native Spaniard as translator and he replied that he wanted to get straight to the owners and would not be giving any money to those smug southern bastards for doing nowt. It almost hurts my fingers to type that word (bastards, not nowt) but the truth must prevail if I am to tell my tale sincerely. (Southern readers should not be too offended as it is just his manner of speaking and he was actually quite friendly with an old workmate of his who was originally from Peterborough.)

That evening we decided to be adventurous and had dinner in a restaurant in Fuentecastillo and had no problem ordering our pizza and chips as the menu was in English. Fuentecastillo is a pleasant place and I said to Ken that although we couldn't afford to buy a house there we might be able to afford to rent one. He said that there was no point getting a taste for it and that he would *not* live in a flat, so that was that. Personally I thought that the mountain village – almost a small town really – was rather isolated, inaccessible and a long drive from the coast, especially behind one of the numerous tractors which some of the locals insist on driving about on. I thought the streets were a bit steep for our aging legs – and neither of us is as slim as we might be – and that it might get rather chilly up there in winter, but I did not wish to dampen Ken's enthusiasm by giving vocal expression to these niggling doubts. If later there would come a time when I could have said I told you so I preferred not to have told him so in the first place and thus avoid upsetting him. So I didn't tell him, but you, the reader, have a right to know, so I've told you.

The following day our third trip to the village seemed even longer than the first two. It appeared that the better we got to know the road, the more interminable all the bends became. Juan was waiting for us at the agreed spot and hopped into the back seat in order to take us to a house up a very steep concrete track some way outside the village. The house was a charming bungalow with a small, still empty, swimming pool and a lot of nice fruit trees. A fat middle-aged man with a deep purply-brown tan came out to greet us and introduced himself as Willy. Willy was Belgian and spoke good English. He seemed to know Juan quite well and explained to us that, apart from this spring trip, he normally only used the house in summer and that he would be prepared to rent it to us from October to June at a very reasonable price. His very reasonable price was quite high but Ken remarked later that it would seem reasonable to someone with a brand spanking new bloody great Land Cruiser on his drive. Willy showed us round the lovely house and Ken listened to him very politely as he described its features, even nodding from time to time. I can only assume that Belgians are not on his list of most hated foreigners which I know for a fact to include Germans, French, Italians, Poles, Pakistanis, Japanese, Argentinians, Africans, Americans and people who live on the Isle of Man.

After telling Willy that we might be in touch we drove down the precipitous track and Ken told Juan that although that house was a bit dear he did like the idea of renting from October to June and would like to see more places where that arrangement could be made. Ken was due to retire from his job at the factory in August, you see, so it did make good sense, although it didn't make much sense to Juan whose

English didn't now seem as good as it had done in the restaurant. This didn't matter too much as the next house he took us to see, up another steep track, was also owned by Belgians, a couple this time, who spoke English and also appeared to know Juan well.

Ken didn't hit it off so well with this couple, who, unlike Willy, spoke English in a French accent and who, according to Ken, 'minced around like a couple of ballerinas'. Their bungalow was very nice, although neither it nor the car on the drive were as posh as Willy's, which led us to expect the price to be cheaper, which it was, but not by much. After viewing the house Ken asked Juan if there wasn't anything a little cheaper and he replied, not in these exact words, that the two other houses he knew of outside the village would probably be dearer still, but that he did know of two in the village itself which he would be glad to show us.

The first of these was the same house with the rubbish dump which we had seen the day before, but the second was somewhat more appealing. It was a large, narrow, three-storey house in the middle of a picturesque, cobbled and very narrow street with a nice little garden to the rear. Juan thought the rent would be quite a bit cheaper than the others we had seen. Prepared for an explosion of wrath at being shown a terraced house – Ken was brought up in a two up two down and once we had bought our semi he swore he would never go back down the social scale – I was pleasantly surprised to find him pleasantly surprised by the spaciousness of the rooms and the charming views from the top floor. Ken asked Juan if he thought that the neighbours would be noisy and Juan held has hands at least a yard apart and said that the walls were so fat, meaning thick, and we wouldn't hear a thing. This house was owned by an English couple who were absent at the time, but had left a key with Juan as they only came out in the summer months. Ken asked him where they were from and Juan said Kettling, which must be Kettering and must be far enough north for Ken's liking as he asked Juan if he had their number, which he had, at home.

On the endless drive back down to the coast Ken said that he bet the swine, meaning Juan, would speak to them first to get a commission out of them, but that he thought that was fair enough as we wouldn't have found the house without him. This I took to mean that we were going to rent the house, which thrilled and worried me at the same time as I thought that we would be rather isolated up there and, judging from Ken's continual grunting down the mountain road, I feared that our trips to the seaside would be few and far between.

After a pleasant dinner in the same restaurant as the night before we went for a stroll along the promenade and at last I had chance to offer Ken a penny for his thoughts, which had been impossible in the restaurant due to him watching football over my shoulder during the entire meal.

"What do you think then, Ken?" I asked.

"What do *you* think, Doreen?" he asked back, which I thought very considerate.

"You tell me first, Ken," I said.

"Let's look into that last house we saw. Nine months would give us plenty of time to see if we like it here and to find a house to buy."

"Should we not have a look down here on the coast too, while we're here?"

"I've told you that I'm not living in a flat."

"Of course not, dear," I said, but didn't say that he had sworn never to live in a terraced house again either. "I'm just a bit worried that we'd be a bit isolated up there in the village."

"We could always stay in England."

So that settled it.

The rest of our stay in Fuentecastillo was very pleasant. The days were sunny but the spring temperature dropped considerably in the evenings, making me wonder how cold it would be up in the village as I had noticed that the house we were destined to rent did not have central heating. I decided not to bore Ken with these trifling thoughts, but the fact that he seemed in no hurry to ring the owners did lead me to suspect that he was getting cold feet, something I feared we would both get in that house in the middle of winter. In this, however, I was mistaken as on our last day he told me that he was waiting until we got home to ring them. His reasoning was that Juan would have rung them straight away to demand his commission before giving us their phone number and that now they'd be waiting on tenterhooks for the phone to ring.

"Let them wait," he said, "and it'll be easier to knock them down a bit. We don't want to sound too keen," he added, which I thought amusing as sounding keen is not one of Ken's specialities.

2

Well, soon after we arrived home Ken rang the couple from Kettering and after a few niceties and a little haggling, which brings out the best in Ken's loquacity, the deal was done and we arranged to meet them at the house on October 1st and to move in with all their furniture, which I remembered as being quite tasteful. I rang them once when Ken was out to ask them how they heated the house in winter. Felicity, the wife, answered the phone and told me that as they had never stayed at the house in winter they had never needed to heat it, but that it was nice and warm in summer, even at night. I asked if they had ever stayed at the house in spring or autumn and she was adamant that they had not, but I felt sure that she was lying, though it pains me to say so. Thankfully for Felicity I have changed her name, though when writing about the first weeks of winter there I was sorely tempted to use her real name *and* surname, but I see I am getting ahead of myself again.

The next question on our minds and my lips was what to do with our house in England. I was all for putting sheets over the furniture and just waiting to see if we liked it in Spain, but Ken reminded me that we were not rich and that we'd better find somebody to rent it before we left. Given the fact that we had made this decision I was all for calling a reputable estate agent to find us suitable tenants, but Ken said he was damned if he would pay the money-grabbing sods to do something we could easily do ourselves.

I must confess that I found the idea of letting any Tom, Dick or Harry live in our house quite disturbing until Ken had the brainwave of me putting adverts in all the local schools in order to find a teacher or teachers to rent the house during the school year. This seemed to be a good idea as teachers tend to be educated, studious and sensible people and a week after traipsing round all the schools we got a call from Michelle, a geography teacher, who was keen to rent the house for herself, her partner and their two children. I supposed that the offspring of a teacher were more likely to be well-behaved and respectful of other people's property than normal children so I agreed with Ken that they ought to be exemplary tenants. I will say more – much more – about this later.

The next thing we had to do was to break the sad news of our emigration to our two children, Susan and Ken (Jr.), and to Ken (Sr.)'s mother. We decided that a dinner to celebrate Ken's 65th birthday – on July 14th, although the dinner was on the 16th – would be the best time to do this. While I was rinsing the dessert dishes and putting them in the dishwasher I was racking my brains as how best to break the news to them, but I needn't have worried as when I returned to the lounge Ken had already told them.

He had said, he told me later, 'We're going to live in Spain from October. It's a little terraced house miles from the sea and there's no swimming pool,' which I suppose was one way of not getting our grandchildren's hopes up. They all took the news quite well considering the shock it must have been and only Ken's mother, Edna, said she was looking forward to coming out to visit. Visit she must, I thought, and she did, but she'll not be getting any Brussels sprouts, which she did in the end too.

So as the house would be fully furnished, expect for heaters, and we would be leaving ours fully furnished for the teacher's family, the only thing we had to do was sort out any necessary paperwork. I looked through my Spanish book collection and found that in some cases this business had hardly been mentioned while in others the process of getting identity cards had been fraught with obstacles and many meetings with mostly colourful and eccentric officials. I rang Juan, who we had stayed in touch with, and he said it was no problem as he would introduce us to a nice Swedish lady who would guide us through the process for a modest fee, which gave me considerable peace of mind on that score.

When I told Ken that it was quite a complicated process which one of the books I read said involved driving to Malaga at five in the morning to queue up he became enraged and said since when was a British passport not good enough, especially seeing as any European could fly here and be signing on within the week. In an attempt to sooth his ire I said that we should be thankful that we were not buying a house yet as that process was incredibly time-consuming, but this had the opposite effect to the one I intended and it was almost a relief to hear the door slam as he left for the pub. Red tape and bureaucracy have never been among Ken's strong points.

Our last English summer was a wet one, for a change, and while I continued to work in my part-time job at the bakery, Ken was at home coming to terms with being retired. He had always hated his job at the factory, as he often told me over the years, so I expected him to be much happier now that it was over, but not being a man of many hobbies – none, in fact, unless you count watching football, visiting the pub and mowing the lawn – he did seem to struggle to fill the time. I suggested that he read some of my books about Spain and I set aside half a dozen of the best ones for him. Imagine my surprise when I returned home from work one afternoon to be greeted by the news that he had finished one of them!

The one he had finished was the thinnest and least good of the good ones and it turned out that when he said finished he really meant 'finished with' because after fifty pages he had chucked it onto the settee in disgust. When I asked him what it was that he didn't like about it, he said could I not see that the writer had turned every character into an angel, freak or eccentric – and herself into a mixture of all three – and that there was no way that all the boring things she had done could have thrown up so many weird characters. I challenged Ken on this point, as I often stand my ground, and asked him why on earth she would do such a thing.

"To sell books, obviously," he said, "because if she wrote the truth it would be like watching paint dry. Imagine someone coming to live in England," he went on, for retirement did seem to have made him more talkative. "They'd find somewhere to live, get a job, try to meet people. Do you think it would make a good story?"

"It might," I said defiantly.

"It might if a lot of unexpected things happened, but nine times out of ten it would be *boring*. So how come everybody who moves to Spain seems to step into a drama? I could see through that one straight away," he concluded, pointing to the offending object on the settee.

"Try this other one, then," I said, undaunted. "This is definitely true."

"I might, but I think it'd be more useful if we spent some time reading this," he replied, and to my utter and complete astonishment produced a small book about the Spanish language.

"Ken!" I exclaimed. "Are you going to learn Spanish?"

"Well, I'm not saying I'm going to *learn* it exactly," he said a little sheepishly, "but it'll be a damn sight more useful to know how to say a few things than reading a load of tall stories."

This initiative of my husband's left me speechless, so I said nothing, but while I was making the tea I had to admit to myself that, what with one thing and another, I hadn't thought about learning the language at all. On all our holidays over the years we had always got by in English, but it did occur to me that if Juan, for instance, was a translator and couldn't speak English very well, how badly would people who weren't translators speak it? There might even be people who couldn't speak it at all and then where would we be? In the books about Spain, you see, all the conversations are in English with just the odd Spanish word thrown in for effect. It suddenly dawned on me that what that meant was that *all* of those conversations – most of them hilarious, ominous or tragic – had actually been in Spanish!

After putting the Shepherd's Pie in the oven I returned to the lounge and found that Ken had gone out to the garden for a smoke. I picked up the language book and to my great relief found that the first page was in English. That first page promised that after studying the book you would be able to get by in Spanish in most everyday situations. Encouraged, I turned the page and started reading about the way Spanish letters were pronounced – they have a funny 'n' with a squiggle, and a double 'L', but then so do we – and then something about verbs. I opened the French windows and asked Ken what verbs were and he said that they were 'doing words', which left me none the wiser.

When he came in from his smoke he must have seen that I was looking very perplexed as he patted me on the head and admitted that he couldn't make head nor tail of it either, but that he had another little book which would be more up our street. He pulled it out of his shirt pocket and handed it to me.

"It's a phrasebook," he said, "full of words and phrases, what they mean in English and how to pronounce them. That'll do us."

After flicking through it I was relieved to find it much easier to understand and Ken said that I should pick up another one at Smith's so we'd have one each.

"Carry that around and you'll never be stuck," he said, and how right or wrong he was the reader will find out for him or herself later in the book.

I said goodbye to my long-time colleagues at the bakery three days before we were due to leave. I would like to have finished earlier but Ken said that we would need every penny we could get, which I thought a little cheeky as I've been drawing my pension for three years already while still keeping on working. Mavis, my oldest colleague and almost but not quite a friend – she sometimes swears without meaning to – said that her and her Joe would love to come and visit us when the weather was nice. Ken's line of, 'It's a little terraced house miles from the sea and there's no swimming pool' proved useful on this occasion and had been well worth memorising.

We sold the car on the 28th of September and booked a taxi to the airport at eleven o'clock on the morning of the 30th. Michelle and her family had agreed to arrive at half past nine to give us just enough time to explain everything and not enough time for me to start worrying about entrusting our property to them. I had wanted to take our bed linen and some of our ornaments and things with us, but Ken said it was just more hassle and expense to arrange delivery and that we would make do with an extra suitcase each. It was easy for him to be nomadic because not having any interests he only needed to take his clothes, shoes and pipes, but I told him that I would jolly well need three of the four suitcases for my things, which he generously agreed to. A lot of our ornaments, pictures, clothes and many other sundry items have ended up in taped up boxes at the back of the garage with 'Do NOT open' written on them. I hoped for our tenants' sake that they would obey these instructions.

Well, all these matters suddenly paled into insignificance when Michelle arrived with her two children and her partner, HELEN. Yes, you have read that correctly because when Michelle mentioned her 'partner' I just assumed they were living in sin, which seems to be quite the thing these days, when in fact Helen, as her name suggests, is another woman.

Ken didn't flinch an inch but when Michelle saw me looking at Helen, then back down the drive to their car, then at Helen again – five or six times, Ken said later – she laughed, a nice feminine laugh, and formally introduced me to Helen as her partner.

Ken showed them the fuse box, the mains water tap and other little things while I recovered my composure and by the time the taxi arrived I think I was managing to speak to them as if they were a normal couple. I slumped into the taxi with great relief and we must have been half way to the airport before it even crossed my mind that we may well have just left the house where we had lived for twenty-four years for the very last time, so absorbed was I in thinking about Michelle, Helen and their children. I sometimes think that Ken has a capacity for mindreading because after twenty minutes of silence he turned and slid his thumb up my creased brow and said,

"The kids are Michelle's by the way, from when she was married to a fella. No miracles or anything there."

The children, a boy and a girl, were eight and ten respectively, which made me hope that they had stopped scrawling on the walls and had not yet started setting fire to their bedrooms with cigarette stubs.

What with all these goings on it was not until the plane took off that I really realised that we were going to Spain, to live, which has reminded me and my pen that this book is supposed to be about our lives in Spain and from now on I promise only to refer to events outside that country when absolutely necessary.

3

When we landed in Malaga it was sunny and quite hot – an auspicious start – and this time we knew where the car rental place was and how to get to the village without the tom-tom, so we were feeling quite 'savvy' already. The Swedish woman who Juan had mentioned and who we had spoken to on the phone several times was already proving to be very helpful. She, Hella by name, had suggested that we rent a car for a week which would give her time to help us to find a cheaper car to rent locally as we wouldn't be able to buy a car until we had sorted out our residence paperwork.

Ken, after another short rant about identity cards, pointed out that this would mean us returning to the airport with both cars to drop the first one off and that I would have to drive one of the cars down to the airport. The idea of driving in Spain did not appeal to me at all, but Ken said that I'd better get used to it if I wanted to get around, which I thought rather ominous as it suggested that he was not intending to get around much at all.

We had hoped to be able to move into the house straight away, despite arriving a day early, so we parked as near as we could and walked up the street in a state of some excitement, me at least. The Kettering couple, who will remain nameless, greeted us politely but regretted that we couldn't move in until the following day. They did deign to invite us in for a cup of tea and the way their things were strewn about the place suggested that they had been there for some time, exploding her myth that they only used the house in summer. Juan later told us that from April to October he had often served them in the restaurant, but that he had only ever seen them once during the winter and that they had looked very miserable throughout the meal and that when the time came for them to leave she had burst into tears and clung to the table.

After our cup of tea without biscuits we returned to the car and drove around the village to the hotel which they had recommended, Ken muttering, 'more expense, more expense', and worse things as he negotiated the narrow streets. The hotel was decent and offered good views of the mountains and the village. Ken said it would be the ideal place for visitors to stay, but I pointed out that there was a spare bedroom in the house. He said it wouldn't take him half an hour to dismantle the beds, before cackling hideously. This cackle usually means that he is joking, but I am never quite sure and this time I was less sure than ever.

The barman who served us drinks and the waitress who attended to us at dinner seemed slightly less miserable than the ones on the coast and they both spoke English at least as well as Juan. Made bold by the wine we had drunk I asked the waitress if she lived in the village and she said that she did. I then asked her if she liked living here and she said that she didn't as it was boring and there was nothing to do. I then asked her if there were things for older people like ourselves to do and she said, no, she couldn't think of anything for older people to do either, but if we had a car we could go to the coast and into Malaga.

Later in the bar I remarked to Ken that what the young lady had said had not been very encouraging and he replied that it was like anywhere else and that you had to make your own fun. For a man with no hobbies to say this made me wonder where and how this fun was to be had, but I concluded that time would tell, which it has, as the reader will see in due course.

Our first full day of residence in Spain was slightly cloudier than the day before and a brisk wind made eating our breakfast on the hotel terrace a chilly affair. After a full English breakfast Ken, between puffs on his pipe, remarked how clean and bracing the mountain air was and I said that it was likely to get a lot more bracing in the coming months and that I hoped we'd made the right decision.

We soon packed up our things and lugged the suitcases to the car and when we arrived at the house we found that the Kettering couple were also packed and after they had taken our deposit, given us their bank details, and made us sign a contract in Spanish they said they must dash. When he had brought the car round to pick up their bags the husband said that the number for the gas bottle man was on the list of instructions stuck to the fridge door under the name 'Butanero', before hopping agilely into the car and driving away.

Intrigued by this gas bottle business Ken hunted around until he found three big orange ones in the cupboards next to the cooker, two connected to tubes and the other not. After further research he concluded that the bottles, or rather cylinders, powered the cooker and the hot water. He also concluded that one being empty and the other two less than half full meant that we would soon be ringing the number that the sneaky bastard – Ken's words – had finally remembered to tell us about. After we had taken the suitcases upstairs and unpacked a few things I said that I'd make us a nice cup of tea, but on finding that there were no teabags, sugar or milk I instead slumped down onto a kitchen chair and burst into tears.

Generally speaking I only burst into tears about three or four times a year and Ken usually ignores me until I stop, but this time he saw that the stress of arriving in our new country and the poor welcome we had received had been too much for me. He patted me on the shoulder before saying that he wouldn't be long and within half an hour he had returned with two shopping bags, one full of essentials and other of bottles of beer. He said that the Tetley teabags he had bought had been so expensive that it'd be cheaper to drink beer and we had a good laugh about that before I quickly put the kettle on. Ken likes his beer, you see, but normally only drinks it at the pub and I don't really want him to start drinking it at home *and* wherever he finds to go out and drink it. It worried me that him not being accustomed to having so much spare time he could take to drink like he did when Ken Jr. was born.

After a refreshing cuppa I felt better and spent the afternoon unpacking my things and placing the framed family photographs in places where I would see them. Ken had unpacked in a jiffy and spent the afternoon sunning himself in the garden – more a patio really – and reading yesterday's Daily Express. Approaching tea time Ken called me and asked me when tea would be ready, but I pointed out that in Spain people don't have tea, or dinner, until about nine o'clock. He said that his organism would need time to adjust but that he would be able to last until about seven today, before returning to the garden with a bottle of beer.

I thought that with it being our first night as residents we might go out for dinner, but it appeared not, so I rustled up what I could from what Ken had bought – I would do a proper shop the next day – and called Ken in. Dinner time is when we normally turn the telly on so, being a creature of habit, I turned it on and took the remote to the round dining table and sat down. The first channels were all in Spanish so I carried on pressing and when I got to about number fifteen the channels became all blank or fuzzy.

"Ken," I said, "I don't think there's any English channels."

"Give it here," he said, and took the remote from my hand. After pressing every button on the device several times he went to mess with the telly before returning to the table and tossing the remote down in disgust. "The sadistic bastards didn't tell us there was no English telly," he growled. "I thought they looked like clever buggers when I saw that copy of The Guardian."

"What will we do?" I lamented.

"What can we do? Go out for a drink," he concluded.

"Without knowing where to go?" I asked dolefully, "I was going to ask Hella about places to go out to tomorrow."

"Where's your sense of adventure?" Ken asked, already pleased that he was going to get some more to drink.

"I haven't got one," I said, not quite truthfully as I was living in Spain after all.

By the time we locked the door and walked down the street it was dark and eerily quiet. After coming out on a wider street where cars would fit, just about, we spied a bar and hastened towards it. It was full of Spanish men drinking bottles of beer and nibbling olives and nutty-looking things and I was just about to suggest that we try somewhere else when Ken saw that there was football on the telly, which is like a red rag to a bull for him. We sat down at a table in the corner and the scruffy waiter – or possibly the owner – came over with a little pad in his hand and started speaking to us very quickly in Spanish. I think he was reeling off a list of food, but Ken soon made him understand that we didn't understand.

"Hold your horses, mate," he said. "Do you serve pints?"

"Qué?" said the man, meaning 'What?' I found out later.

Ken mimicked the cradling of a large glass and utterly astonished me by saying, "Cerveza, mate."

I now know that cerveza means beer, of course, but I was ever so impressed that Ken had managed to say a sentence half in Spanish on our very first outing. The man then pointed to the beer bottles on the next table and Ken said, "Dos of them, then, mate," and was duly rewarded with two bottles of beer, one of which was for me.

Ken took a long swig from the bottle before patting his shirt pocket, wherein lay the magical phrasebook. As I hadn't been brought a glass I took the phrasebook and looked up the word in the little dictionary section at the back, before plucking up the courage to summon the waiter or owner and say, "Vidrio, por favor." Pleased with the 'por favor' bit, which Ken hadn't thought to say, I was soon struck off my pedestal by the fact that the man hadn't a clue what I was talking about.

"Vidrio?" he asked.

"Vidrio," I said. "Un vidrio," I added to clarify, before looking at the page and seeing another word for glass. "Or cristal," I ventured, to the man's increasing amusement. He then popped behind the bar and came back with two glasses which he put down on the table.

"Vaso," he said, pointing to the larger one. "Copa," he added, pointing to the wine glass.

"Ah," I replied, and while I was searching for the word, Ken beat me to it.

"Gracias," he said, "amigo," he added, just to show off. At that moment I resolved never again to leave the house without my phrasebook and I have remained true to my word.

By the time the football had finished there were nine empty beer bottles on our table, Ken having consumed six of them, and I did wish that the owner – I was sure he was the owner by now by his proprietorial manner – would take some of them away. The bar emptied quickly after the final whistle was blown and I said that we'd better go too as we didn't want to start getting a boozy reputation on our first night. We paid at the bar and Ken left a four euro tip, which the owner found both surprising and pleasing.

"Buenas noches," I said, before smiling proudly at Ken. He snatched the phrasebook from me and after flicking through a few pages said, "Hasta mañana," meaning 'See you tomorrow', which I thought a little ominous as he only went out three times a week in England.

Ken brushed his arm against me affectionately on our way back down the narrow street to our house and, all in all, despite the telly fiasco, our first full day in Spain had turned out all right in the end.

I had hoped for a bit of a lie in on my second full day as a Spanish resident, but the shouts of noisy schoolchildren penetrated the single-paned bedroom window and by half past eight I was wide awake, so I got up, which was just as well as at about nine o'clock Hella knocked on the door and said that we had a busy morning ahead of us. Hella is a tall and imposing blonde woman of about fifty and has lived in the village for twenty-two years. I made her a cup of tea while we waited for Ken to get up and I asked her if she was married. She said that she wasn't as she only enjoyed the company of Spanish men during the night, finding them dull daytime companions.

If she intended to shock me by this bold statement, I don't know, but as I was already well aware of the liberal attitude towards sex of Scandinavian, and French, women I took it in my stride. Later that morning when we were walking from place to place I thought I saw a little animosity towards her in the dark eyes of the local women, so she may well have 'played the field' in her younger days, I thought, only to later learn that she *still* played the field even at her advanced age, which I must admit did shock me a little and made me keep my eye on Ken's eyes when she was around, although he's no longer up to much.

The first thing that Ken said to her, apart from hello, was how could we get English telly. She said that we would need a satellite dish and a box and that she would take us to the local supplier after we had carried out the more important business, which was to visit the town hall and to open a bank account. At the town hall the girl behind the desk spoke good English and gave us a form to fill in which she said was to put us on the electoral register. At the bank the man behind the counter spoke even better English and we had soon opened an account and could call in for our bank cards the following week.

Later we went for a coffee on the terrace of a nice café where the waiter spoke good English which made Ken comment, when Hella had gone to the loo, that we hadn't really needed a translator after all and that he hoped she wasn't going to charge us a fortune for doing nowt. I argued that we wouldn't have had a clue where to start, to which Ken replied that what had been the use of reading all those books by people who had moved to Spain then? I said that most of the writers hadn't gone into much detail about it as it would make very boring reading, which makes me now wonder why I am writing it down at all.

Anyway, Hella came back from the loo and took some forms out of her bag which she said were from the national police station at Fuentecastillo and that we had to fill them in, get some passport photos, make some photocopies of our passports and collect together a few more documents which are too boring to mention (one from the town hall, another from the bank and a medical form). Once we had everything ready she would accompany us to the police station at Fuentecastillo to hand it all in, along with a small fee, after which we would soon become bona fide residents.

After our coffee we walked up a very steep street to a sort of electrical warehouse where a man explained to us, in broken English this time, what our telly options were. It transpired that if we wanted to watch all of the English channels all of the time we would have to fork out a whopping great sum of money for a whopping great dish – Ken's words, not the man's – or we could go for a somewhat cheaper option which would allow us to watch some English channels some of the time. Ken said we would think about it, which he did, but more about that later.

Ken then asked Hella about hire cars and we were disappointed to hear that the garage that hired them out in the village wasn't all that much cheaper than the one we had driven up from the airport. Before we parted I asked Hella what we owed her for her services and she flapped her large hand and said we would sort all that out when everything had been done. What with one thing and another Ken and I returned to the house feeling weighed down by impending financial burdens. He took a bottle of beer and his pipe out into the garden while I prepared some sandwiches for lunch and when I took them outside he smiled and said that he had already come up with a solution.

"English telly be damned," he said, and that he'd get Bob to post some DVDs over. "Hire cars be damned too," he went on, as we'd take the car back to the airport and come back on public transport and would buy a car when we (meaning he) were (was) good and ready. Staggered by these radical proposals I almost dropped the sandwiches at his feet before recovering my senses and flopping down onto a plastic chair.

"Ken," I said. "Up here all the time and with no telly we'll end up going native."

"Rubbish," he replied, "but there's no point being here if we're going to do exactly what we'd do in England, is there? We'll have to try to fit in a bit."

"Yes, but… I thought you didn't like foreigners?"

"We're the foreigners here, remember," he concluded.

Not taking kindly to being called a foreigner in my own home, I took my sandwiches inside and ate them in the kitchen. Nor was this to be the end of my husband's revolutionary decisions as when we later made our way to the supermarket and did a weekly shop his response to the bill was,

"And English food be damned because we can't afford those stupid prices," before making me put back the Weetabix and buy the inferior Spanish cereals that we've been eating ever since.

On sitting down to dinner at seven o'clock I instinctively turned on the telly and on finding a channel where the adverts weren't on I furtively observed Ken's reaction to the future he seemed determined to condemn us to. Being as stubborn as a mule, of course, he had to stick to his guns and he pretended to follow the programme about the goings on in different Spanish villages with interest. I protested that he couldn't possibly understand a word and he said that he got the gist and that it would eventually sink in. After dinner we sat down in the lounge – there was a decent settee and two of those Ikea easy chairs – and I began to feel at a bit of a loss. I mean, the telly being on did give the room a familiar feel, but not being able to understand it made me think about the programmes that would have been on had we had English telly. I suppose that's what comes of watching it most nights for the last fifty years, but Ken could see that I was suffering and asked me why I didn't read one of those books about Spain that I was so keen on.

Heeding his kindly advice I went to fetch the one I was reading and turned to the page I was on. The man who wrote it had just had a hilarious conversation with some colourful people in a shop and then met up with an eccentric old man who he wanted to buy a goat from. It was amusing to read but seemed a far cry from us two sat in our rented house in a godforsaken village and not knowing a soul, unless you counted Hella and Juan.

I did cheer up though when Ken said that it would be fun tomorrow to drive down to Malaga and then make our way back here on the bus. I'd read about lots of entertaining bus journeys in the books and thought that perhaps tomorrow we would have one of them, before I remembered that I'd realised that all those conversations were probably in Spanish, as was the one I was then reading involving the crazy goatherd. I lay the book aside and asked Ken what we could do and he replied that he didn't know what I was going to do, but that it was Wednesday and he was going out.

"Can I not come?" I asked.

"It's Wednesday," he replied. "My night out."

"But we could both go out," I pleaded.

"On a Wednesday? You've never been out on a Wednesday, except once when we were courting."

"But everything's changed now, Ken. We're in Spain."

"Wednesday's still Wednesday whatever country we're in. I won't be late," he concluded, before picking up his pipe and wallet and leaving me all alone.

Other books about Spain have their sad moments between all the amusing and exciting ones and that was a very sad moment indeed for me. I wandered about the house and out into the garden and felt like a princess, though quite an old one, trapped in her tower. At that moment I must admit that I wished we had never left England, but the reader should not worry, or even cast the book aside, as I promise that these low points are few and far between and I think that this was one of the worst of them.

Ken came back just after eleven looking very rosy and seeming a bit tipsier than usual. He said that he had been to the same bar as the previous night and had watched the football and got on very well with the locals. I asked him if they spoke English and he said that they didn't, but that he'd got by just fine with his phrasebook and a lot of gestures. His pipe then clattered to the tiled floor and I said that it seemed that he had drunk more than usual. He said that his usual four pints were equivalent to seven bottles and that that was all he had drunk. I shall have more to say on this subject in the future.

As I lay awake in bed listening to Ken's placid snoring I resolved that I too would have to meet people and I decided that I would let no opportunity to do so slip me by. While Ken wasted his time with his illiterate football chums I would build up a network of interesting friends, and I finally coaxed myself to sleep thinking these positive thoughts.

4

The next day was another sunny one and over our breakfast of cheap cereals and not very nice milk I put on a brave face and said that I was looking forward to the drive down to the airport and our adventurous journey back on public transport. After all, if we were to become temporarily (I hoped) carless it would be as well to know how to catch the bus down to the coast.

Ken was even less talkative than usual and I felt sure that he was suffering from a slight hangover due to the total of nine (that I knew of) bottles of beer that he had consumed during the evening. He has never been a lush – apart from the six month period after Ken Jr was born – and I reasoned that he would soon adjust his intake when he realised how strong Spanish beer really was. My cheerfulness over breakfast more than made up for his muteness and I resolved that when I had made a host of interesting friends I would share some of them with him when he had tired of his barfly buddies.

The drive to the airport went smoothly enough and it was with some regret that I said goodbye – figuratively speaking – to the hire car and we plunged into the unknown. It turned out that there were buses *and* trains into the city and I urged Ken that we take the train to give variety to the journey. The nice clean train started off underground but soon surfaced and sped towards Malaga where it went underground again. Most people got off at the second to last stop and instinct told me to follow all those people with their rucksacks and suitcases, but Ken said that there was one more stop in the centre and that is how we overshot our destination and, to add insult to injury, Ken's ticket would not work and we couldn't get out. After the fourth try there was no-one left around us and I feared that we were destined to spend the day in that inhospitable bunker, until he saw an intercom button and pressed it.

A female voice squawked out of it and Ken told her that we couldn't get out. Ignoring the fact that he had spoken in very clear English, she rattled off a short reply in Spanish and hung up. Ken was all for clambering over the turnstile, but I warned him that we were not residents yet and could end up locked up in a cell with a lot of illegal immigrants. He pressed the button again and said 'English, please' before repeating our predicament. This time she squawked on for a little longer before hanging up and Ken had begun to haul his ample frame onto the barrier when another train arrived in the nick of time and a kindly Scotsman told us that there was another exit at the end of the platform where they would let us out.

When we came face to face with our intransigent tormentor, who was as fat and ugly as she had sounded, she showed no remorse at having subjected us to that ordeal and after looking at the ticket and shrugging, let us through and waddled back to her chair. When we surfaced from the station we found ourselves in the centre of a strange city with no idea in which direction to head. Ken's solution was to ask every single passer-by if they spoke English, including an ancient lady dressed all in black who averted her face before crossing herself, and at the fourth attempt a young man responded in the affirmative before giving us directions to the combined train and bus station that we had should have got off at.

After twenty minutes and three more interrogations by Ken we finally found the station and I slumped down onto a bench in relief. Ken had survived the ordeal with more fortitude and went to buy the tickets, returning twenty minutes later in a similar state to myself. It turned out that there were several ticket offices, each selling tickets for different bus companies. The information office had pointed him to the one with buses for our village and after queuing up he had been told that the next bus left in two and a half hours, upon which he had asked for tickets to Fuentecastillo, which that office did not sell, so he'd had to queue up again and now faced me brandishing the tickets with a murderous gleam in his eye.

"Are we in bloody Africa, or what?" he exclaimed, drawing annoyed looks from several bystanders, before heading for the bar.

We both drank two nerve-steadying beers while we whiled away the hour before the bus was due to leave and the hour-long journey passed without incident, expect for Ken wanting to go to the loo and finding the door locked, provoking another comparison with the Dark Continent, but mercifully more quietly this time. I had visited the bathroom before we left the station and so was in a more relaxed frame of mind and I noticed that some other passengers did indeed make conversation across the aisle, just like in the books, but none of them seemed out of the ordinary and they all spoke in Spanish so I couldn't join in.

When we alighted at the tiny bus terminal Ken made a beeline for the toilet and on his return we made a mental note of where we were, before heading through the town to the sea. After sitting on a bench on the pleasant promenade for half an hour and congratulating ourselves on how well we had coped with all the obstacles thrown in our way we returned to the bus terminal in good time to catch the bus up to the village.

That the bus was late did not worry us – Ken said he had expected no less – but what did soon become a cause for concern was that there was nobody else waiting for one. After a while I went into the little office to ask and after naming our village I received a torrent of words, a lot of pointing and finally, on the unpleasant man seeing my perplexity, a card for the 'Oficina de Turismo', or tourist office. On reaching this office a pleasant man who spoke good English told us that the bus to our village belonged to a different company and left from a different street. He hunted around for a timetable and was sorry, he said, to tell us that we had missed the last one of the day, before kindly offering to call a taxi.

Ken asked him how much a taxi would cost and he said that he thought it would be about fifty euros. I think it was only the fact that the man had been so helpful that stopped Ken from going through the roof, something he later did in fact do after we had paid off the taxi and stood in the centre of the village seventy-five euros poorer.

"The robbing bastards," he said, more loudly than I would have liked. "That's the last time I'm getting into a sodding taxi in this country," he added, and to this day he has stuck by his words.

When I had steered him past the bar and back to the house I took the bus timetable from my purse and noted with relief that there were three daily buses down to the coast and three back. That evening as I read my book and Ken pretended to watch telly I fingered the timetable, which I was using as a bookmark, and felt reassured that I would not be trapped in the mountains after all.

The morning after that very trying day we awoke late and I suggested to Ken that we go to one of the nice cafes for one of those mid-morning breakfasts that I had read so much about in the books. He agreed and after climbing slowly up our shadowy street and along another one we emerged into the square and after taking our seats sat basking in the sun while we waited for the busy waiter to attend to us.

"This is the life," I said.

"Yes," Ken agreed, puffing his pipe serenely.

"What would we be doing now in England?"

"You'd be at the bakery and I'd...," and his voice tailed off in the realisation that he wouldn't have been at the factory, but at home and with nothing to do.

"What'll we do today?" I asked.

"Oh, just take it easy and enjoy the weather," he replied, which is what he later did.

Ken, when the weather is nice, has a capacity for sitting in the sun with his pipe for hours on end, reading the paper, or just meditating, I suppose you'd call it, although he wouldn't. In this respect, retirement to Spain is perfect for him, but I'm not like that and I prefer to be busy or around other people. With this in mind I looked around the terrace as I ate my toast with jam and drank my café con leche, wondering who I might strike up a conversation with. All of the other customers looked foreign, by which I mean not Spanish, and there were several couples, who I did not wish to intrude on. Fortuitously for me, one couple left the table at our side and a thin, middle-aged lady sat down in their place. I guessed that she was English by her hair, curled like mine, her face, and the fact that she had a Daily Mail sticking out of her bag.

"It's a lovely day," I ventured.

"Yes," she said, looking at the sky. "The days will be all right for a while, but the nights will soon start getting chilly."

"Do you live here?" I asked.

"Yes, worse luck," she said sadly in her pleasant singsong voice which I later found came from Devon, or rather she did. Undiscouraged by her discouraging statement, I strove to continue the conversation.

"We've just moved here," I said.

"Did you buy or are you renting?"

"Renting."

"Thank goodness for that. You can get out when you want. I've been trying to sell my house for the last two years."

With Ken's tacit approval she moved over to our table and introduced herself as Shirley, a retired dental nurse from a village near Taunton, and told us her story. It transpired that on losing her husband – to another woman, not to death – she had sold up and moved here four years ago, wanting to avoid the hubbub of the coast and hoping to learn the language.

Things had seemed to go all right at first as she had studied Spanish and taken every opportunity to practise in the shops and cafes, but it was only when she started to really understand what people were saying and was able to ask more searching questions that she realised, she said, that they didn't want to know.

"Know what?" I asked.

"Know me; better, I mean," she replied. "People are pleasant enough here on the surface but deep down they don't like foreigners living here. It's not a big place and we've pushed up the house prices and now the youngsters can't afford to buy. I'm not well off, but there are plenty that are and the locals resent them and their swimming pools and big cars. The same thing has happened in Devon so I know where they're coming from. Grockles – tourists, that is – are all very well but you want them to clear off after they've spent their money. Now I want to sell up and buy myself one of those nice little apartments down on the coast which were mostly built for us foreigners in the first place."

"Oh," I said, taken aback.

"Was there no mention of what Shirley's just said in any of them books you've been reading?" Ken asked me with what I felt was a hint of playful malice in his voice.

"No," I replied.

"No, I suppose not. Wouldn't make very good reading, would it?" he said, rubbing salt into my mental wounds.

"If I wrote a book, it'd be a short one," said Shirley. "Perhaps fifty pages about the first year and another ten about the next three. I'm bored to death here. I don't want to put you off though. It might be different for you, and being a couple you've always got each other's company."

"Yes," I replied doubtfully. "Have you got English telly?" I then asked.

"Oh yes, if I didn't have that I'd go stark raving mad."

"We haven't got it and Ken says we're not having it," I said, feeling that I may have made an ally.

"Oh dear," said Shirley. "What on earth will you do on the long, cold winter evenings?"

"I don't know, Shirley," I said, observing my husband out of the corner of my eye. "I really don't know, but we're planning to buy and we don't know where yet."

"I'm not living in a flat," said Ken.

"Oh, but some of the apartments on the coast are lovely," said Shirley to my delight. "They've got nice lifts and all mod cons and I'm sure you wouldn't have a witch for a neighbour like I have here."

Shirley then went on to tell us that while on one side of her there were some Germans (wince from Ken) who hardly ever came, on the other lived an old widow who never spoke to her.

"She never speaks but she stares at me with her beady eyes from under her black scarf. I think she's trying to give me the evil eye. What are your neighbours like?"

I said we didn't know yet and it was true that neither of us had given a thought to who our neighbours were. In our semi back in England we were on helloing terms with those on either side of us and on nodding terms with one of the couples opposite, but in most of the books I had read about Spain it was very different. The writers usually became close friends with at least one of their neighbours and any cranky ones were depicted humorously and were quite harmless. I suppose there is some humour to be had from being given the evil eye by an old crone, but then the reader doesn't have to see them every day.

This mention of neighbours made me determined to pay ours a visit with my phrasebook as you never knew; they might well be our passport into the social life of the village. We said goodbye to Shirley and said we hoped to meet again soon and wandered back towards the house, Ken buying a Daily Express on the way which he took straight into the garden while I put the kettle on. Buoyed up as I was after making friends with Shirley, I decided that it was a good time to pay the neighbours a visit, so took Ken his cup of tea, picked up my phrasebook, and left the house.

I knocked on the door of the neighbours to our right and waited nervously for someone to appear. When the door opened and a sleepy looking teenage boy appeared I said 'Hola', which means hello, and wished I had prepared something else to say from my phrasebook. Fortunately the boy spoke some English as after an uncomfortable pause he said, "Yes?" I explained that I was the new neighbour and without replying he disappeared into the house and called 'Mamá' which I correctly guessed to mean mother, or rather mum. After a while a dark haired, dark eyed, but surprisingly pale skinned woman of about forty appeared and gave me an enquiring glance. Assuming this to be an English-speaking, or at least English-understanding, household I said that I was her new neighbour and that me and my husband Ken had just moved in next door. She looked at me blankly and it occurred to me that the boy had been rather thoughtless to leave me to my fate before his monolingual mother.

Undeterred, I resorted to mime and pointed to our house and then to myself. Spurred on by her slight nod of comprehension I pointed to myself again and told her my name, at which she nodded again but did not divulge her own. I then pointed to my wedding ring and at the house and said 'Ken', and she nodded again. Feeling the conversation was at an end I said 'Adiós', which she responded to in kind before closing the door. When I returned to the house for a rest before tackling the neighbour to our left, I realised that I had not made any use of the phrasebook, but I somehow doubted that it would have made the conversation much longer. Perhaps it was because she knew that her bad-mannered son would never be able to leave home due to us foreigners pushing up the house prices that she hadn't been friendlier.

After swotting up a few things from the phrasebook I went out again and knocked on the other neighbour's door. This time an old, wrinkled lady opened the door and stared at me in a most disturbed and disturbing way. Feeling that she was unlikely to speak English I introduced myself and said 'vecino', meaning neighbour, and pointed to our house. She just continued to stare and I started to feel that I had met her before until I realised with a small thrill that she must be Shirley's neighbour. The thrill produced a big smile on my face which frightened the woman, who backed away muttering under her breath before slamming the door in my face. Overjoyed – not by having the door slammed in my face, but by my discovery – I made a beeline for the next house where, sure enough, Shirley answered the door.

We met like long lost friends and I said well I never and she said who'd have thought and I see that the excitement of remembering the excitement of our meeting has made me forget all about speech marks and things. She invited me in – something that, had we not been neighbours and knowing what us English people are like, might not have happened for weeks – and put the kettle on, saying what a small world it was. I agreed and before long we were sitting outside in her garden – more of a patio really – chatting away over our cups of tea.

Although I am as honest as the day is long I am not averse to a little scheming and I saw that I could turn Shirley's experience in the village and her intention to move to the coast to my advantage, especially due to the fact that Ken must have thought she was all right, despite her southern birthplace, as he had listened to her politely instead of rudely looking away or at the ground as he is wont to do when he takes one of his instant dislikes to someone.

We laughed long and hard about my discovery of our mutual neighbour, long and hard enough to send Ken's voice over the two high garden walls with a 'Who lives there, Doreen?' I shouted back that it was Shirley's house and he said it was a small world and I was about to say something else when a piercing howl came from the house in between, meaning, I surmised, that the old witch did not approve of us shouting over her coven, if that's the word, and we had a hard job to stifle our laughter so as not to offend her even more.

I mentioned to Shirley the unfriendly reception I had received at our other neighbours' house and she said that the lady I had met was all right really but that her husband spent most of his spare time in the bar and that her son, who was eighteen, had finished school, couldn't get a job, and spent his days smoking 'weed', something that a lot of the youngsters of the village seemed to do. A little shocked to hear that drugs were available in such an out of the way, rural place I asked if they came from Colombia and how people could afford them if they weren't working. Shirley laughed at my naivety, because I have *never* touched drugs myself and nor has Ken, and told me that they grew it themselves and that the local police couldn't care less.

After tutting sympathetically, because it'll be a shame if all the youngsters start to die off, I changed the subject back to the one that interested me, namely collecting information to help convince Ken that we'd be far better off living down on the coast. Shirley said that after she had given up trying to make any real friends in the village she had taken to catching the bus down to Fuentecastillo at least once a week and had also visited other coastal towns. There, she said, although there were plenty of Spaniards, there were also enough British people for them to have clubs and societies which did different activities, arranged trips and so on. Here in the village the foreigners were from all over the place and tended to do their own thing. Some of them were a bit snooty too, she said, as they had more money than was good for them.

She went on to say that what with the economy picking up a bit she had finally had some interest in the house, which had prompted her to start viewing apartments in and around

Fuentecastillo, and she was hopeful that she'd only have to survive one more winter in the village.

"At least I've got a good wood burning stove which keeps the downstairs warm," she said.

"We haven't," I lamented.

"What have you got?" she asked.

"The only thing I've seen is a little fan heater in the bathroom."

"Oh dear," she sympathised. "You'd better get something sorted out then."

"Ken says it can't be that cold in Spain."

"We're high up here, you know."

"I can tell by the road," I replied.

"It doesn't often freeze but it gets very chilly at night. The mountains look lovely covered in snow."

"That'll be nice," I said, and I was sure it would be, but always having been prone to cold feet, even with carpets and central heating, this news was very worrying indeed and the only consolation was that Ken would suffer too and hopefully see the light.

I hoped that Shirley didn't move to the coast too soon as I felt that I had made a real friend, but, on the other hand, if she did we could visit her and Ken would see how sensible people lived. So with all these pros and cons floating around my head I said goodbye to Shirley and returned home to find Ken already drinking a bottle of beer. I pointed out that it was a bit early to start drinking and he said that he hadn't 'started' drinking but that beer was so much more refreshing to drink when sitting in the sun than tea, adding that it made him feel like he was on holiday.

Seeing his point, I poured myself a small glass and began to tell Ken about my conversation with Shirley, at which he raised his hand and said that he wasn't deaf and had heard it already. He then said, in a low voice, that just because she hadn't found the village to her liking didn't mean that we wouldn't. In fact, he said, the neighbour had just popped round and given him some onions, garlic and carrots and that the bag was in the kitchen. Astonished, I asked if it had been the elderly neighbour and if so that we shouldn't eat any of it as she may well be a witch. He said, no, it was the neighbour on the other side and I said that I had just called on her and that she hadn't even given me the time of day.

"No, the bloke," he said. "I got friendly with him in the bar. He's called Pedro and he's got an allotment."

"Shirley says he spends most of his time in the bar," I said.

"The bar in the evenings and the allotment at the weekend. He likes to get out of the house."

"His poor wife," I said.

"Spends all day watch telly according to Pedro."

"How did you understand all this?"

"He remembers a bit of English from school. With that and the phrasebook we make a do. No need for any of this grammar business."

That evening we were both getting fidgety by about eight o'clock so Ken went to the bar and I went round to Shirley's to watch a bit of telly. Was this a sign of things to come? The reader shall see in due course.

5

The next day being a Saturday the schoolchildren didn't wake us up, so we got up late again, just before ten. I warned Ken that we shouldn't get into slovenly habits and should start to set the alarm, but he said that he'd been getting up early since he started school sixty years ago and that it was about time he took it easy. This talkativeness and relative good humour reassured me that he hadn't drunk too much in the bar the night before, but the good humour soon came to an end when the water went cold just after he had soaped himself in the shower. I won't repeat the words that he yelled and which carried down into the kitchen and probably half way down the street, as although this book is truthful there is no need for gratuitous vulgarity.

When he had emerged from the shower looking very rosy from the cold water and all the sunbathing he'd been doing he inspected the gas bottles and found, of course, that two were now empty and the other one – the one for the cooker – didn't have much left in it either. He said it was all a bit primitive and I said that I bet that down on the coast they had a proper gas supply. He said that he was not living in a flat, which seems to be his answer to any comments made about the coast, and that we'd better ring the gas wallah and get him to bring some more bottles round. I rang the number hoping that they would speak English, but I needn't have worried because there was no answer.

I then popped round to see Shirley, who I found in curlers, and she told me that we'd have to wait until Monday to get hold of them, so I returned home expecting more fireworks, but Ken was unperturbed as he said he could make do without another shower until Monday and it was me who'd have to have a cold one, but that he'd found his very invigorating. Seeing my crestfallen face – my hair really was due for a wash – he laughed and said that it would be quite easy to change the bottle over while I had my shower. Much relieved and keen to capitalise on his good humour I suggested that as it was Saturday why didn't we go out to dinner at the restaurant where Juan worked and he said it was a bit dear but agreed.

I agreed that it was a bit dear, but pointed out that with the cost of living being so low here, according to the books, we could afford to eat out sometimes. He agreed, again, and said that one good thing about not having a car and not paying for stupid satellite TV meant that we'd have more money to spend. While on the subject of transportation I said that it would be nice to get the bus down to the coast one day next week, for a change, I added.

"What? And end up getting another bloody taxi back?" he said gruffly.

"No dear," I replied pleasantly, "I've got a timetable and when we get off we'll see where the bus stop is."

"They might change it again during the day," he replied facetiously.

"Well I'll go with Shirley then," I retorted quickly.

"You do that. She'll appreciate that if she's got no friends."

"Friends aren't easy to make here, Ken," I pointed out.

"No? Well we've only been here a few days and we've both made one already. Pedro's going to take me up to see his allotment tomorrow. I might help him out a bit sometimes. It'll keep me fit."

Although I hoped that we weren't going to end up having separate lives, I didn't begrudge him his new friendship, though he hardly knew this Pedro and the man might have an ulterior motive for befriending his foreign neighbour, perhaps thinking him rich and influential, though I must say he doesn't look it, especially in the old vest he wears continually around the house and garden.

As Ken intended to spend the whole day in the garden and Shirley was going to be busy with her hair for some time yet, I decided to go for a walk around the village to explore. Until then I hadn't strayed very far from the centre so I decided to walk right up to the top of the village and then meander back down right to the bottom. The narrow cobbled streets were very quaint, but very steep indeed, and after a few minutes walking I had to stop, both to catch my breath and to avoid breaking out into an unsightly sweat. I soldiered on, however, and eventually reached the top, where some new houses had been built and I found a bench to sit down on.

I had counted the number of times I had said 'Hola' to people and out of nine 'Holas' from me I got five replies, the other four just staring at me blankly. I think this compares quite favourably with England, but I still felt a bit disappointed. When people ignore you in England it is because they are ignorant so and sos, but here I feared that it was because I looked foreign, meaning not Spanish, and they thought I had come to buy up all their houses causing their children never to leave home. When I later mentioned this to Ken he said that I was being paranoid, but that his policy was never to say hello to anyone, so that if anyone greeted him it was a bonus.

Walking back down through the village was hard work too as the steepness, combined with me being slightly overweight, put a lot of pressure on my poor old knees, so much so that I decided to leave the lower half of the village for another day. The village is picturesque, it is true, but I couldn't help thinking that the towns on the coast would seem a good deal flatter in comparison. Perhaps when Ken had walked around, or rather up and down, the village a bit more, I thought, he would come to realise this state of affairs.

When I arrived home I was more than ready for my shower and hair wash so I asked Ken to spare a moment from his sunbathing to connect the hot water. He had no difficulty in swapping the gas nozzle onto the cooker bottle, but it took him ten minutes to light the pilot light of the water heater, amid more foul language and references to Africa, which seemed a bit daft as I doubt they have many gas bottles at all in the middle of the jungle. Ken told me I'd better make it a quick shower as there wasn't much gas left and proceeded to make it the worst shower and hair wash of my entire life by standing outside the bathroom door and repeatedly telling me to hurry up. He had me in such a state that I wasn't sure I'd got all the shampoo out of my hair as it felt a bit strange when I was putting my curlers in, though that might just have been the different water, which has never agreed with my fine grey hair, but I digress.

When my curlers were in, it occurred to me that perhaps we should invite Shirley along to the dinner that evening and Ken, by now looking extremely red in the garden, did not object, as long as she paid her way. I popped round to ask her and was careful to phrase the invitation in the right way, as follows:

"Shirley, would you like to come along to dinner with us tonight at the restaurant just off the square?"

"Yes, that would be nice. What time?"

"Shall we call for you at eight?"

"That's fine."

I reproduce the full conversation because when I returned to our house Ken asked me what I had said, so I told him.

"She'll think we're paying," he said grouchily.

"I don't think so," I replied and, after reliving the conversation in my head several times in the course of the afternoon, to this day I still don't think that it suggests for a moment that we were offering to pay.

Anyway, by a quarter past eight Shirley, myself, and a very red Ken were seated in the restaurant while the friendly Juan stood poised with his pen and pad. We ordered our meals (steak for Ken and lamb chops for me) in English, of course, but Shirley ordered her swordfish in Spanish and was disappointed when Juan repeated her order in English and said, 'Thank you, lady'. This, she said when he had gone, was the trouble with trying to learn Spanish in a place where all the young folk were trying to learn English, and Ken replied that it would be even worse on the coast. Shirley said that she didn't mind that, as if English was the 'lingua franca' down there that was fine with her, but up here where half the people don't speak a word of it, the other half make it blinking difficult to learn Spanish, and nobody *ever* corrects you, she added with what I thought was a touch of venom.

Ken, talkative after his afternoon swilling beer, said that she'd probably paid too much attention to all this grammar business which he thought just confused things. She agreed that he might well be right and for the rest of the meal we talked of other things very pleasantly and all got along very well together until the bill arrived. Ken being the man, he took the bill and said that €77 was very reasonable considering all that we'd eaten and drunk. Then there was a pause in conversation while Ken slowly took his wallet out and began, even more slowly, to count out four €20 notes. When the last of them were on the little tray Shirley thanked him and said that it had been a lovely meal. Ken nodded and during the twenty minutes or so that it took us to take our leave of Juan and saunter back down our street the only word that passed his lips was 'Bye', which he said, he said, so as not to be rude.

Once inside the house he said he'd be damned and if the cheeky cow hadn't taken us for a ride. I said she must have misunderstood and after Ken had made me repeat my 'invitation' four times, which is probably why I remember it so well, he passed judgement.

"No," he said, patting me on the arm. "You said it all right. She's a sponger and that's all there is to it. That's why she's got no friends."

I said that she would probably invite us to lunch or dinner sometime and he said that if she did he'd eat his baseball cap, the one that I'd dug out for him to protect his balding head.

"Once a sponger always a sponger," he concluded, before belching disagreeably and taking his pipe out into the garden.

This put something of a damper on an otherwise pleasant evening and how right or wrong Ken was in his aspersions the reader will find out in due course.

The next day, a Sunday, Ken went to meet his new friend Pedro at the bar at ten o'clock and returned home just before nightfall looking and acting distinctly like he had 'had a few'. I first suspected that he had just spent the whole day in the bar, but his burnt shoulders, apart from where the vest straps go, proved that he had indeed been outside for much of the time. Not wishing to be accused of nagging, however, I made no reference to his somewhat inebriated state. I asked him if he had had a good day and he said that he had, but that he'd done a lot of clearing, picking and lifting and that he felt tired out.

"Lifting a lot of beer bottles, by the look of you," I said, forgetting momentarily that I wasn't going to nag.

"It's thirsty work," he replied.

"There is a thing called water, you know," I responded ironically.

"Well, it was a Sunday," he replied, whatever that meant, before going into the garden with his pipe.

He hadn't mentioned tea, or dinner, so I wasn't going to mention it either, but being bored in the house I finally went out and asked him if he'd had any. He had, he said, had a bite to eat in the bar on the way back, which Pedro had paid for unlike some people he could mention. He then said that as Pedro worked during the week he had kindly agreed to lend him his old moped so that he could pop up there if he felt like it and do a bit of planting.

I said that this Pedro would have him working for nothing and he replied, 'au contraire', which proved he was tipsy, and that I should look in the hall at the box of vegetables that he had given him already. I went to look and found the box full of more onions, garlic and a few carrots and then asked Ken what he expected me to do with all that, especially the garlic as none of my recipes contain the foul stuff.

"That's all there is just now," he said, "but we've started planting turnips, peas, broad beans and radishes, and I'll be getting my share of them. Anyway, I'll only be popping up there when I feel like it."

After breakfast the next day, a Monday, it turned out that he already felt like it and he asked me to make him some butties to take with him as he might get peckish later. I told him that I had nothing pressing to do and could come with him, but he said that the old moped only had one seat, something I saw to be true when he sputtered past later with a silly little helmet on.

"If we had a car, I'd be able to come too," I said.

"Yes," he replied thoughtfully.

"We can get one when our papers are in order. We're going to Fuentecastillo with Hella tomorrow, remember."

"Oh yes," he said, looking disappointingly disappointed.

"The police station won't take long and then we can have a wander round," I said encouragingly.

"Don't even think about showing me any flats," he growled.

"Of course not," I said with a smile, preparing him for the next thing I was going to say. "Shirley's going to come too, for the ride."

"Well she'll not be taking me for another ride. She can pay for her own bloody food."

"Of course, dear," I said, hopefully.

"Speaking of food, how about those butties?"

"I'll make them now."

"And don't forget to ring the gas bottle bloke."

"I won't, dear," I replied, which I did, so by the afternoon we were back up to full capacity.

Ken was back by six, looking redder than ever – he says he'll go brown eventually – and mercifully did not smell of beer. He brought some shrivelled peppers to add to our store of mostly useless vegetables and ate his Shepherd's Pie voraciously, washed down by three bottles of beer. It was true, like he said, that the exercise would do him good, but I did start to wonder what I was going to do with myself if he was going to start going to our as yet unknown to me neighbour's allotment all the time. I won't say that the reader will soon see, as I see that I've said that quite often already and it stands to reason that the reader will see as that is the nature of books.

6

At nine o'clock on the following morning, an unusually dull one, the four of us squeezed into Hella's little car, Ken in the front of course, and set off for the coast. We kept up an animated conversation as we wended our way down the windy road, all except Ken, who was busy picking skin off his peeling nose despite my protestations. Before we had left the house he had given me the notes from his wallet and had left his change on the table, saying that it was my responsibility to ensure that Shirley paid her way.

The police station business went very smoothly, unlike in the old days, as Hella and some of the books said, when the authorities made it very hard work for foreigners to come to live and spend all their money here. Now they seem to have seen sense as it is the foreigners who keep the economy going in coastal areas, Hella added in that slightly superior Swedish way of hers.

Free from our bureaucratic duties, we gravitated towards the seafront where Hella said there was a nice bar to have some 'elevenses'. We all ate a 'bocadillo' – a sandwich on local, unsliced bread – and drank pop, water or beer (Ken) before ordering coffee to finish off with. I started to feel very tense when the time to pay approached and I eyed Ken nervously as he scratched at his rapidly pinkening nose more frantically that ever. The sullen waiter brought the little tray and, him being the man and this being a macho society, left it on the table in front of Ken.

Ken pushed the tray into the middle of the table, slightly nearer to Shirley than anyone else, and lit his pipe. Under normal circumstances I would have pulled the bill from under the clip to have a look at it, but with Ken's eyes peering ominously at me from within a cloud of smoke I hesitated. Shirley cunningly chose this moment to ask Hella if she wouldn't prefer to live down on the coast and the two of them were soon gabbing away – in a contrived way, I thought – about the pros and cons of village and coastal life. Although I was pleased that the pros of coastal living were easily winning the day, the presence of Ken, now puffing so furiously that he was completely enveloped in a dense fog, made me so nervous that I broke out into a cold sweat, so instead of joining in the conversation like I should have done and just leaving the bill where it was, I found myself taking it from the tray and unfolding it. The presence of Hella made the matter more complicated as I reasoned that she might have reasoned that we should pay for her because she had driven us here to help us sort out our paperwork, something that had proved unnecessary, again, as the young lady who had attended to us had spoken excellent English. Then I reasoned that if she was going to charge us for all the 'work' she was doing there was no reason for her not to pay her way, before thinking that making her pay might make her simply up *her* bill by another ten or twenty euros. Then, as they rattled on about beaches and bistros and Ken sat grimly submerged in his smog, I tried to divide the amount into four in order to boldly tell Shirley how much her share was, but by that time I was in such a tizzy and the bill was getting so damp in my hand that the figures just whirled around in my head and I couldn't make the calculation to save my life.

So, fearing that I was going to have a panic attack like the one I had when our Susan brought home a black boyfriend (Ken soon put paid to that business) I opened my purse and thrust a €50 note and the bill back under the clip and rushed off to the bathroom, where I bathed my face and waited for my heart to stop thumping alarmingly. When I returned to the table, by then feeling so limp that I almost didn't care what had happened, I found them all standing up and ready to go. On seeing Ken's expression and noting an absence of warlike fury on his face I assumed that either Hella or Shirley had paid, or that they had paid between them. It later transpired that Hella had said that she would pay for us two, as it was 'all part of the service', thus audaciously forcing Shirley to cough up €7, which Ken said had been a joy to watch and almost made up for the fact that the Swede was bound to screw us in the end.

I think that this financial wrangle put something of a damper on our little party as after that no-one seemed to know what to do or where to go, so Hella drove us back up the mountain amid desultory conversation and dropped us all off at the end of our street. The next day Hella posted a pretty little envelope through our letterbox which contained an official looking itemised bill for her services which came to €121, twenty-one of which were for sundry expenses, meaning the elevenses. When Ken had almost finished cursing her he remarked that she'd been bold enough to make the bloody southerner pay up, but too embarrassed about ripping us off in that sneaky Scandinavian way of hers to hand us the bloody envelope. He added that we'd make her wait a bit and that if she came round when he wasn't in to say that I didn't have the money on me.

After tea he said he was going to the bar, which he did, and left me alone to ponder on the day's events. It certainly seemed to be more stressful living in Spain than I had anticipated and I almost longed for the tranquil evenings in England when we would each sit contentedly watching the telly, unless it was one of Ken's three nights down the pub which now appeared to have turned into four or five. Putting the events of that testing day down on paper proves that you don't need escaping animals, flash floods or hailstones the size of footballs, like in some of the other books, to create high drama. Not if you are married to Ken, anyway.

The next day, a Thursday, Ken said that he felt like popping up to Pedro's allotment as he hadn't been for a while – a whole two days – so he puttered past on the moped and left me to my own devices once again. Feeling at a loose end I realised that after harping on about Ken not having any hobbies that I didn't really have any either and that now with this allotment business he *did* have one. My first thought was to pop round to Shirley's to ask her if she had any hobbies, but that reminded me of all the stress of the day before so I didn't go and instead took a cup of tea and a pen and pad out into the garden and sat down to think about the different things I could do.

Straight away I realised that one thing I missed was not going on the internet. In England we had the internet because, and only because, it came with the telly package and that although I'm no expert I could look up things – mainly about Spain – on the little folding computer that Ken Jr. had lent me. I decided that I *must* have the internet, and a computer to use it on, or on it, in order to stay in touch with the outside world and search for a suitable hobby. I also reasoned that if I couldn't find a proper hobby that way, at least 'surfing' the internet was a sort of hobby in itself and I could find out how things like that face book worked and keep in touch with people back home, or what used to be home until a week ago.

My excitement at discovering my hobby or means to a hobby soon diminished, however, when I remembered that I would need to gain Ken's approval. The fact that he considers the computer age to be a complete waste of time and can't imagine why anybody would want to be in constant touch with anybody else, coupled with the fact that he dislikes spending money, made me realise that he would be a tough nut to crack in this matter and that I had better make sure that when I laid my cards on the table that I knew the approximate price of each of the cards.

To do this I would have to seek advice. My first thought was to look things up on the internet and I laughed at myself for thinking this, for obvious reasons. Who, then, could I turn to? Hella was out of bounds, of course, as she would want to get her grasping hands on her money and I still didn't feel like approaching Shirley due to the traumatic events of the day before. Who then? As Juan the waiter was the only other person I knew, if you don't count the neighbours, and I didn't, I made the audacious decision to go to the restaurant for lunch *alone*.

In England I probably had lunch, or dinner as it was then called, in a cafe four or five times in my whole life, but this was Spain and I even wondered if it was the done thing for a lady to lunch alone. Throwing caution to the wind I decided to risk it and the two hours until two o'clock – the correct time to have lunch in Spain according to the books – passed even more slowly than my last winter in England, relatively speaking of course, as I paced around the garden thinking about the pending experience and Ken's possible reaction to it, on top of me wanting a computer.

Well, the time finally passed and after putting on a nice skirt and blouse I walked up the street and along to the square, before dawdling for a while to make sure that Juan was working, which he was, so I went to take my seat at one of the outside tables and nervously played with the paper tablecloth until he found time to take my order. At another table there was a foreign but not English couple eating a paella and all the other diners were inside and must have been mostly Spanish judging from the racket they were making, and the language they seemed to be speaking. It was quite chilly in the October shade, but I preferred to weather the cool weather than face the multitudinous eyes of those inside.

Juan finally emerged with his pen and pad and after greeting me warmly asked me if I wanted the 'Menu del Dia', or daily menu. I had read about the wonders the Menu del Dia in some of the books, where for eight or nine euros you could stuff yourself silly and not have to even bother with dinner or supper. Here I saw that it cost €11, because of inflation and the fact that the village is full of foreigners, I suppose, but it was still a lot cheaper than their evening prices, especially if Shirley tags along.

After very self-consciously eating the thin soup and very dry chicken – nothing like their evening fare – and ordering a flan for dessert, I decided that the time had come to pop Juan my questions about computer matters. When he brought the tiny flan I asked him where I could buy a not too expensive computer and he said that if I wanted a new one I should go to Fuentecastillo, but that his sister had a nice laptop that she wanted to sell. I asked him how much she was asking and he thought for a while before saying €150, which made me think that he had added a bit on for himself, or why would he have to think about it? I mean, he would know the price or he wouldn't, wouldn't he?

I then asked him about the cheapest way to get the internet and he said that if I wasn't going to be using it all the time I should get myself a dongle. I begged his pardon and he explained that a dongle was a little thing that you plug into the computer and that I could get one at the local electrical shop for about €30. He didn't need to think about this so he must not get any commission there. I said that it sounded a very reasonable price to get the internet and he laughed and said that I would also have to put money on it which I could do in the shop or at the bank.

I thought about all this during the minute it took me to eat my flan and when he later brought me my café con leche he said that if I wished he could bring his sister's laptop and his little brother's dongle to the restaurant and we could try them out. I asked him how many brothers and sisters he had and he said three – without hesitation – and that his house was very noisy. I then asked him when he was going to get his own place and he shrugged and said that he couldn't afford it, which made me wish I hadn't asked as it is people like me who have pushed the house prices up, so I shouldn't grumble if he makes a little extra money however he can. It is ironic that the very people who are giving him his daily bread with one hand are taking away his chance to get a place to live with the other.

While he was getting the bill I think he was also doing a bit of mindreading as when he returned he asked me if we were happy in the rented house and if we had started to look for one to buy yet. I said we were happy in the house, which was at least half true as Ken seemed to like it, but hadn't decided where we wanted to live yet, exactly half true as my heart was set on moving to the coast. He replied that he would let us know if any more houses came up for sale in the village and added, after penetrating through my glum expression into my brain, that his cousin worked in Fuentecastillo and sometimes heard about apartments being sold cheaply.

He interpreted my mingled look of hope and resignation correctly and said that although he was very happy that I lived in the village he thought that I would be happier on the coast as there was nothing to do here and the weather was better down there, especially in winter, particularly at night. I reminded him that Ken refused to live in a flat and that he had become such good friends with our neighbour and spent so much time at his allotment that I feared that he was getting very settled here. Juan asked me who the neighbour was so I told him his name, at which he pulled a face and, having been called back into the restaurant, said he would return shortly. (He didn't actually say, 'I will return shortly', of course. All of Juan's side of this conversation has been reconstructed from his pidgin English. Translator my foot.)

When he returned he asked me if Pedro had said anything to Ken about a house that he was selling. I replied that I didn't think so and asked him which house he referred to. I will now allow Juan to speak.

"Is house he mother. She dead and he want sell. Very old house and bad roof. Dangerous electric. Wet walls in winter. He look for foreign people to buy. No village person buy. It is a shit. You not buy," he concluded, waving his finger and looking very serious.

I thanked him for sharing this with me and agreed to come to the restaurant the next day at about twelve o'clock to try the computer out. As I walked home I began to feel very pleased with myself. I had had lunch alone, I was a step nearer to getting the internet, and I had some very useful information which I decided to store away until it could best be unleashed on my gullible husband.

Ken returned at about six smelling only very faintly of beer and with the white parts of his nose already taking on a bit of colour again. He said that the cooler weather had made it very pleasant to get on with the planting and that when we bought a house it would be nice to have one with a bit of land to grow things on. I agreed that it would, envisaging some nice window boxes on our apartment balcony, and resisted the temptation to ask him if Pedro had mentioned a house. I chuckled to myself mischievously as I made the tea and would await the day that he burst in with the news that his 'friend' Pedro just happened to have the ideal house for us, before passing on Juan's information, with embellishments of my own, and watching his face change from one of trusting friendship to one of murderous hatred. Ken does not take kindly to being deceived. He is a man of extremes and I trusted that his fury would not only focus on the no good neighbour, but on the whole village and that our move to the coast would then be plain sailing.

7

Pedro, I thought, must be cleverer than he looked – I had seen him by then and he didn't look very clever at all – because a week went by without Ken mentioning any mention of a house for sale. Pedro must have been biding his time and I would have to bide mine, but I was sure that news of the house would not be long in coming.

By now we had our bank cards and our residency papers and, above all, I had my little computer and dongle which helped me to while away the time. The evening after my solo lunch at Juan's restaurant, and making the most of Ken's good mood after his day spent planting things that he will never eat, I told him about Juan's sister's computer and said I wanted to buy it to be able to go on the internet and stay in touch with people because, as he had correctly pointed out, Shirley was not much of a friend after all. I made no mention of the fact that I'd need a dongle as I assumed, correctly, that he was so clueless about computers that he'd think that it picked up the internet just like that.

He asked me how much it would cost and I said €180, adding a bit on for the dongle anyway, but that perhaps I'd be better off in the long run buying a new one, which would cost around €500, another slight exaggeration. I said all this in a very serious way and the contrast in prices had its desired effect. He still grumbled, of course, but as he is a fair man deep down and as he clearly intended to be at the allotment most days and in the bar most evenings, he said that I should buy Juan's sister's one, which I did the next day, along with a dongle from the electrical shop.

In the following days I read all I could about Fuentecastillo and the surrounding area, especially things regarding English people there and, of course, the latest house prices. I stumbled upon things called 'blogs', in which people write about what they have been up to. My first thought was that I could write one myself, but then thought that I would wait until I was down on the coast and actually doing things, rather than spending most days reading about what other people were doing. This was proving quite expensive as €10 on the dongle soon goes if you spend as much time 'surfing' as I did, but rather than putting money on it at the cashpoint, I did it at the shop out of my housekeeping money. Ken had not complained yet about the simplicity of our meals, but he never really notices what he eats anyway.

Man and woman cannot live on the internet alone, however, and a couple of days after getting the computer I paid a call on Shirley as, although she is not up to much, she is the nearest thing to a friend that I have got here. She seemed pleased to see me – it wasn't me who made her spend the €7 after all – and we soon got chatting as if nothing had happened, which I suppose it hadn't really. I told her about the computer and she told me that she too spent a lot of time on the internet, staying in touch with her friends on this Facebook thing that I kept coming across. She said she had over two hundred friends, which seemed a lot for such a mean person, but, when she showed me, I saw that by 'friends' she included people who had been to school with her daughter's boyfriend and things like that – not what you would call close friends at all.

Anyway, by inviting her home to lunch I asked her to get me started on Facebook too and, after eating her fill, she showed me how to put some photos on and search for friends. Our Susan couldn't believe it when I got in touch with her and was very impressed with my computer skills. She told me to follow her friends, so I did, and eight of them followed me back, so with them and the local butcher (in England) I then had ten friends and counting. I searched for people who I had been to school with, but my generation is not very computer savvy and I only found two, neither of who I remembered at all, but they still followed me back. Ken Jr takes after his Dad and doesn't bother with things like that, Susan said, so I couldn't follow him.

One morning I decided to test Shirley out and suggested that we went out for a coffee. As expected, when the time came to pay, her eyes went all misty and distracted so I had to cough up. Her meanness is so severe that I think it probably has a medical name, though I don't know it, and she is a great disappointment, but not nearly as much of a disappointment as Pedro will be to Ken when the house business finally rears its ugly head, I thought.

Anyway, what with spending so much time on the internet I didn't write nearly so many notes for my book, this book, and for the next couple of weeks things went on much the same as before. Ken sputtered off to the allotment most days and went to the bar four or five nights a week, although I was glad to see that he soon got his drinking back down almost to pre-Spain levels and stopped coming home in far tipsier states than can be good for a man of sixty-five.

On one of his days off from exploiting himself at the allotment I persuaded him to take me for a Menu del Dia lunch at Juan's restaurant and by choosing their home-made stew and a more substantial dessert managed to end up feeling a bit fuller than last time, but nowhere near as full as in some of the books. Over coffee who should we see walking across the square but Hella, who we had managed to avoid until then, once by simply ignoring her knocking and slightly irate helloing through the letterbox.

She smiled as she approached us, but it was a frosty Scandinavian smile and as she bore down on us from a great height Ken raised his finger as if remembering something and took out his wallet. Seeing him do this, I invited her to sit down and once the cash had been counted out right down to the 121st Euro she relaxed a little and accepted my invitation to have a coffee. I told her about my getting on the internet and she asked me how I was connected. I told her by dongle and she winced and said that they were expensive to run if you went online a lot. I said, no, no, I only went on from time to time and from then on I would have to curtail my computing in Ken's presence or he would start asking questions. I then told her – because Ken was in one of his less talkative moods, as usual – that Ken had been spending some time at our neighbour Pedro's allotment and kicked myself in mid-sentence as, if she knew him, she might mention the house he was trying to foist off on some foreigner, which would anticipate the events that I was anticipating.

She did know Pedro, it turned out, and, with a dreamy smile on her face, said that he was a 'vigorous man' and 'very discreet', which I took to mean that she had had, or was having, extra-marital relations with him, or rather him with her. I tutted in an amused sort of way and looked at Ken to see his reaction to his friend's deceitful behaviour, but his face registered no reaction whatsoever, so he probably hadn't even been listening. Still, I thought, it was more fuel to my fire when the time came to expose our treacherous, libertine neighbour.

After drinking her free coffee, Hella asked us if we had settled into the house and if we had thought about buying yet. Before I had chance to open my mouth, Ken had sprung back to life.

"The house is fine," he said quickly, "and we're not in any hurry to buy," he added, speaking, he thought, for us both.

"Well when you are, just let me know, because I will be able to help to find you one here or on the coast," said Hella in her precise, cold, mercenary way.

"I'm not living in a flat," said Ken, again.

"That's what I always thought," replied Hella, "but I'm thinking that it might be time for me to move to a nice apartment in Fuentecastillo."

"Really?" I asked, all ears.

"Yes, I'm not as young as I was and the cold winters are starting to bother me. Also I think I have exhausted the possibilities of the village."

"Does it get very cold here in winter?" I asked eagerly, ignoring her sordid innuendo.

"Oh, it doesn't often get below zero, but I'm getting tired of always having to light the wood burning stove. There is no need for one of those on the coast, it is so mild."

Resisting the impulse to kiss her long, bony hand, I replied quickly,

"We only have a little electric fan heater, in the bathroom."

"Good gracious!" she exclaimed. "You will *die* of cold."

I looked through Ken's smokescreen and caught a glimpse of a flicker of concern.

"What will we need to get?" I asked, hoping it would be expensive.

Hella replied that wood burning stoves were quite expensive and were not something you could carry around easily from house to house due to their great weight, so the best option would be to get at least one gas heater, and an extra bottle of 'butano' (gas) to use in it.

"They are a little smelly," she added, "but are not dear and you can take it with you to your next house or apartment."

"One of those will do us for this house or any other *house* we might move to *here* in the village," replied Ken conclusively.

After Hella had taken her leave and was safely out of earshot, Ken shook his head and put his pipe on the table.

"She's no good, that Shirley's even worse, and Juan… well, he's all right but he's always on the make. Pedro's the only one you can trust round here."

"Yes, dear, I suppose you're right," I replied, smiling indulgently and consoling myself with the thought that the time I was biding was a lot easier to bide now that I was connected to the internet.

As October ended and November days ticked away things went on much the same, with Ken spending a lot of time at the allotment and in the bar, and with no sign of us getting a car. Although by that time I had over fifty Facebook friends and had even joined some groups who talked about how wonderful Spain was, I was becoming impatient with our neighbour Pedro who had not yet mentioned the hovel which I hoped he would try to sell to Ken. I saw Shirley now and again – I could get a cup of tea out of her in her own home, but dare not venture out with her for fear of eating into my dongle funds – and it had been a long time since I had been to the coast. One Monday, after checking the bus times and the weather forecast, I told Ken that I intended to go down to the coast the next day.

"What do you want to go down there for?" he asked, as he put his allotment butties into his little knapsack.

"Because I want to see the sea and the shops," I said, "and it's going to be four degrees warmer down there," I added, because the weather had already turned nippy and Ken was almost ready to admit that we would have to get a gas heater.

"Well I'll come too then," he replied, much to my surprise.

"Really?"

"Yes, it'll be a change. I'll see you later on."

As the puttering died away after the moped had strained to carry Ken's slightly reduced weight up the street – the allotment was keeping him fit, like he had said, despite all the beer – I rushed to switch on my computer and plan the following day's trip. This, I knew, was a once in a blue moon chance to impress my husband with the advantages of living on the coast and I didn't mean to waste it.

After 'surfing', or 'googling' as Shirley calls it, for a while to find a restaurant with a good Menu del Dia for €10, I had another look at apartments for sale just in case Ken should bring the subject up, though I knew this was highly unlikely. Then, like a flash, it occurred to me to write 'allotments Fuentecastillo' in the little box and to my immense surprise and pleasure I saw that, not in Fuentecastillo itself, but in other towns down the coast there *were* allotments for rent, as well as some communal ones, and the information was in English! The word 'apartment' may not be in Ken's dictionary, but I reckoned that the words 'apartment with an allotment not too far away' would be a different matter and I spent the rest of the morning making notes of where the allotments were, how much apartments cost near them, and other interesting facts, until my dongle ran out and I made myself a tuna salad.

As I ate my salad sitting in the sliver of sun which still made it into the garden I even considered us catching another bus along the coast to one of those towns, but decided that it would be too much to ask of Ken, especially after our bad experiences on buses, and that I would have to content myself with breaking the news to him at an auspicious moment during the day and hope that the word 'allotment', or even 'an allotment of your own' would work its, or their, magic on him.

8

The day was a bright one, but I hoped that the chilly wind that hit us as we rounded the corner to the bus stop would have become a benign breeze by the time we reached Fuentecastillo and thus score me my first brownie point of the day. The bus was a nice comfortable one, more of a coach really, and about half full. The other passengers were a mixture of young folk, chattering ladies, a few rustic old men, and two middle-aged foreign couples whose strangely purple tans and blue eyes suggested that they had started life as very pale-skinned people from the upper reaches of Europe.

I was pleased to find that it was no worse going down the torturous road in the bus than in a car, and no slower as the tractors are the same for everybody, it being a road where overtaking is well-nigh impossible. In well under an hour we were dropped off on a street where there wasn't even a bus stop and Ken made me write down the name of the street and double check the time of the returning bus, which I did willingly as I wanted nothing to spoil the day, which missing the bus certainly would, with bells on.

As we gravitated towards the sea I remarked to Ken that there was a nice, warm breeze and he agreed that there was, but that the air wasn't as pure as in the mountains, probably due to the fact that we were walking past some traffic lights where there were several cars revving their engines. We had about five hours altogether and I didn't want Ken to be bored or annoyed for a single minute, so I suggested we first go for a coffee at a seafront café, as sitting in the sun with his pipe in his mouth he is never bored and rarely annoyed.

The sun was well placed in the sky for my purposes, as facing it, as Ken was, he was looking along the front with a view of both the sea and the first row of apartments, where a few probably foreign people could be seen reading their papers or just relaxing. I sat facing the sea and was careful not to disturb his trance-like puffing as I wanted the pleasant sight of what the future could be like to penetrate into his subconscious mind. After almost half an hour, however, and with our coffee cups long drained I felt it was time to break the silence.

"Those flower boxes look nice on those balconies, don't they?" I ventured.

"Hmm," he replied, exhaling a cloud of smoke. "You can't eat flowers though," he added, before looking pointedly out to sea.

"Look, there's a man fishing over there," I said, remembering that when we were courting he used to go fishing on the canal on Sundays to avoid coming to my house for lunch, or dinner as it most definitely was then.

"Hmm, if he catches anything I'll buy it off him and eat it raw, scales and all," he replied wittily. "The bloody Spanish have fished the Med to death. That's why they're after our fish now, and everybody else's."

Ignoring an indignant stare from a young man at a nearby table, Ken called the waiter, asked for the bill and paid it, all the while keeping up a patter in what sounded to me like fluent Spanish.

"Ken!" I exclaimed, "When did you learn to say all that?" I asked, flabbergasted.

"Oh, from talking to Pedro and in the bar, you know," he replied modestly.

I kept my feeling of almost insane envy to myself and decided that with him basking in his prowess the time was ripe to play my trump card, but I had to lead up to it.

"How is it going up at Pedro's allotment?" I asked innocently.

"All right," he replied. "Most of the winter stuff is planted now so we just potter around and pick a few weeds."

(And talk and talk with your Spanish friend while I sit at home alone and if I do try to speak Spanish in the shops or with Juan at the restaurant they just reply in English, I thought bitterly, but I managed to keep my raging jealousy out of my voice.)

"Wouldn't you like to have an allotment of your own, though?" I asked nonchalantly.

"I suppose so. Pedro does rattle on a bit when he's there at the weekends and it'd be nice to have a bit of quiet, but they don't really do allotments up there. You buy a field, or a parcela as they call them, or nothing. Too expensive, too much hassle and too much land for me," he concluded, relighting his pipe after his long speech.

"There's lots of allotments near the coast, you know. It says so on the internet," I said as calmly as I could. "Would you like another coffee or something seeing as we're so settled here?" I asked.

"Go on then," he answered. "I'll have a beer."

A beer at this point was just fine by me and I decided to have one myself too. I called the poker-faced waiter over and said,

"Dos cervezas, por favor," exactly as I have written it here, to which the waiter replied,

"Two beers, OK."

"*Why* did he answer me in English, Ken? I get that all the time in the village shops."

Ken asked me to say cerveza again, so I did, and then he said cerveza and told me to say it like that and not as if I was speaking English. After about my sixth attempt he said that was better, so when the waiter arrived with the bottles, I said,

"Gracias para la cervezas," at which he just nodded.

"Gracias *por las* cervezas," corrected Ken smugly and, although I was close to tears through frustration and jealousy, he then said what I'd been wanting him to say. "Allotments, you say? Near the coast?"

I told him that purely by chance I had stumbled upon a 'website' about... well about the next town up the coast, and that nearby there were allotments for rent and all the information was in English.

"Hmm," he said, and sipped his beer.

I then told him that at the next town along there was a collective allotment, run, it seemed, by foreigners.

"Ah," he said, and lit his pipe.

"And at a town along and inland a bit I've read something about free allotments for the unemployed and retired people, run by the council, I think."

"You just stumbled on all that?" he asked drolly.

"Well, no, I stumbled on the first one and then looked into it in a bit more detail," I replied nervously. Had I said too much? I awaited his next words with bated breath.

"Let's go for a wander along the front after this," he said, and nothing more.

"Would you not like to have a look at some of the shops?" I asked.

"No," he replied.

"Not even the gardening shop I think there is about three streets along?"

"No, let's just walk for a bit."

"Yes, let's," I agreed, because it was, after all, about him getting a feel for the place and anyway, the 'gardening' shop I had looked up I found out later was actually a place where people buy the things they need to grow illegal drugs, so he wouldn't have liked that at all, being dead against drugs of all kinds.

It was certainly pleasant to walk along the nice promenade in the sun and watch the waves breaking gently on the empty beach. When we reached the end of the prom Ken suggested walking on along the beach for a bit, to which I gladly consented.

"I bet you could walk for miles along here," I said after a long but pleasant silence.

"It'll be chock-a-block in summer," he replied, "and full of screaming kids, I bet."

"Yes, but most of the year it's not summer, is it?

"I suppose not," he replied.

"The daytime temperature hardly ever drops below fifteen degrees here and it can get a lot colder up in the village, and close to freezing at night," I said informatively.

"How much time have you been spending on that blooming computer of yours?"

"Oh, not long. Shall we turn round and walk back?" I asked, keen to keep both his feet and brain moving.

"Yes, I'm getting a bit peckish," he replied.

We didn't talk much on the way back up the beach and the prom, not at all in fact, and having practically memorised the street plan I soon found the restaurant where we were to have lunch. We sat down at a table outside, Ken taking the chair in the sun, and I prayed that the meal would be good, and I mean literally prayed, and it had been a long time since I had done that, not being very religious minded, but not a total atheist like Ken, who says that 'after this there's nowt' and things like that.

It was a Spanish-owned restaurant, I think, and the waitress who served us was quite pleasant, which was a good start. She brought a salad and gave us English menus which we read carefully before Ken amazed me by ordering his food in Spanish and then looking at me. I ordered mine meekly in English and I swore that I saw the waitress's look of surprise and admiration turn to one of 'business as usual' boredom, but it may have been my imagination playing tricks on me and I put all jealous thoughts out of my mind as I began stabbing bits of lettuce.

Ken took my fork off me before drenching the salad in oil and vinegar, adding salt, and then moving it all around with both our forks. It was the Spanish way, he said, which I never thought I'd hear him say in a month of Sundays. If he had seen himself then a few weeks earlier, he wouldn't have believed how much he had embraced the Spanish language and customs, and neither would I. I always thought it would be me who would make the effort to get to know how things were done and I swore that once we had moved down to the coast I would get my skates on and start practicing every day with my phrasebook.

All these thoughts passed through my mind as I watched Ken stabbing all the olives onto his fork – he wouldn't touch them before – and when I saw that he had ordered *squid* for starter my amazement was complete. I saw that there was a grave danger that he would go native on me if I didn't get him away from that village soon, but I felt I had said enough for the time being and did not disturb him as he popped the foul, rubbery rings into his mouth and chewed them thoughtfully.

The Menu del Dia was nicer than the one at Juan's restaurant and his grunt of satisfaction on finishing his main course of lamb chops – bigger and juicier than the ones in the village despite being on the coast and further away from wherever they raise the lambs – and his silent enjoyment of the generous portion of ice-cream assured me that the meal had been a success.

"What a lot you get for ten euros," I remarked as we strolled away to have coffee nearer the front, it not being included in the price.

"Hmm, but you couldn't do it every day, it'd ruin us," he replied.

"No dear, but once or twice and week would be nice."

"What? And the bus fare on top of that? Not on your nelly."

Seeing that his thought process had not reached anywhere near the point that I had hoped for – either that or he was trying to catch me out and quash my hopes – I did not pursue the matter and instead guided him skilfully to another café with tables in the sun and let him ruminate over his coffee, which he followed up with two bottles of beer – a reassuringly unSpanish thing to do – before it was time to catch the bus back to the village, where I was pleased to find a distinctly chilly wind in the air.

While Ken was in the bar that evening I reflected on the day's events and decided that on the whole it had been a success, as I have enjoyed very few days out, if any, with Ken in all the years that we have been together without there being some irate outburst at some point or another. I decided that I must now bide my time and let him come to his own conclusions.

The next day I was delighted to awake to the sound of heavy rain as it would provide such a contrast to the previous day's summery sensations. While Ken was in the bathroom I switched on the computer to look at the weather on the coast in the hope that it would be sunny down there, but it wasn't, so I just had to hope that Ken's memories of the day before would seep into his brain as he mooched around the house like a lost soul.

Perhaps he would picture himself down on the coast, puffing his pipe and watching the rain fall onto the rough sea from our apartment balcony or from a sheltered café terrace. If he did he didn't say so, and what with not wanting to while away the day on the computer lest he quiz me about the cost, it turned into a very long day indeed, made longer by the fact that I was constantly hoping that he would ask me something about the allotments, or properties, or anything else to do with the coast, at which I would have sprung open the computer like a woman possessed and found him any information he desired.

After tea he complained that he was fed up of being stuck in all day and said he was going to the bar. Resisting the temptation to point out that that would make three nights in a row, I waved him a cheery goodbye and settled down with my computer to search for any enticing titbits of information with which I could build on Tuesday's good work. I 'googled' to find any clubs or societies that he might like, but most of them were in towns on the other side of Malaga – to the left, or to the right looking from the village – and the only one I could find in the towns with allotments was a Fine Arts Society which I didn't think would be his cup of tea at all.

No, I decided, there was nothing to do but wait. Wait for the weather to get colder and wetter so he couldn't putter off to the allotment, wait for the intense boredom of the village and the boringness of the villagers to sink in through his stubborn skull, and, above all, wait for the dratted Pedro to drop the clanger of trying to sell him his mother's decrepit house.

9

The following Tuesday, by then thoroughly fed up of waiting, I told Ken that I was thinking of going down to the coast on the following day. I decided to put it like that as it had made him decide to come the last time, but this time he just said 'Ah' and went off to the allotment. I think the dejection of my day saw itself reflected in the slightly burnt cottage pie which I presented to Ken at dinner time, but after eating a forkful he said something that instantly lifted my spirits.

"Bloody hell, this is like eating coal. It's a good thing we'll get some decent grub tomorrow down at the seaside."

"Oh, are you coming too?" I asked with feigned calmness.

"Too right I am," he said, picking a burnt bit out of his mouth. "The forecast's good and it's nice to get down there."

"Yes," I replied chirpily.

"Once in a while," he had to add, Ken being Ken, and after eating all the edible bits he went off to the bar.

That Wednesday's trip to Fuentecastillo was very similar to the one of the week before as the weather was good and we went to exactly the same places and did an identical walk along the promenade and the beach, turning round at what I could swear was exactly the same spot. Ken is a creature of habit and I was more than happy for him to habituate himself to spending time on the coast, but there was no mention of the possibility of us living there and when we got off the bus back in the cold, lifeless, unfriendly village I had begun to fear that these occasional trips to the oasis of Fuentecastillo, with its friendly people and balmy breezes, were all that he desired.

When we entered the cold, uninviting house I said to Ken that we simply must get a gas heater, as having the fan heater pointing at my feet and whirring away while I tried to watch the Inspector Morse DVDs that his friend Bob had finally posted from England was beginning to drive me mad. He said that he doubted that it would get much colder and I said, oh yes it would, and offered to show him the monthly temperatures on the computer, an offer he declined with a short grunt. If I'd had a printer I'd have pinned that chart on the bathroom wall for him to see when he did his necessities every morning, but a printer was one luxury I had put out of my mind until I had my heater – a sad state of affairs for someone who'd had central heating for over thirty years.

As we settled down to watch an episode of Inspector Morse, all of which we knew off by heart, he asked me if I really needed to have that blasted fan heater buzzing away all the time and I replied that I did because, as he well knew, I was very prone to cold feet. He offered to lend me a pair of thick socks and was telling me where I would find them when I began to sob quietly. After the lovely day at the seaside to come back to this squalor and misery had been too much for me and I stifled my sobs as well as I could lest I disturb Ken's viewing.

He patted my arm and said, "There, there," and when a conversation between Morse and Lewis had ended he asked,

"How much are them gas heaters, then?"

"€114.99, at the electrical shop," I replied, because I had often window-shopped there.

"Hmm, I bet they're cheaper in the big supermarkets down on the coast. We don't want to be spending any money on this house," he said.

"But we can take it with us wherever we go, Ken."

"I didn't know we were going anywhere," he replied, which brought on my tears again.

Ken considerately stopped the DVD and turned slightly to face me.

"Are you not happy here, then?" he asked.

"No, I'm bloody well not," I wailed, which I promise the reader is the one and only time I blaspheme in this book, so please don't slam it shut.

"Where do you want to live then?" he asked patiently.

"On the coast, in an *apartment* if we can't afford a house," I answered with some force. "Why do you think I've been spending hours on the computer reading up on allotments for you?"

"Ah," he said. "Not in the village then? Pedro mentioned that he had a house for sale, you know."

"Did he?" I asked, drying my tears in anticipation.

"But he said that it needed a lot doing to it and that he'd rather sell it to some stupid guiri than to a friend like me."

"What's a guiri?"

"A foreigner the locals don't like, like most of the pillocks who've come to live here. Open that machine of yours then."

"What for?"

"To have a look at how much it costs to rent one of those bloody apartments."

"Oh, Ken!" I almost sang, before hugging him.

After shaking me loose he turned off the telly and went to fetch two bottles of beer while I switched on the computer and quickly found the website that I had pored over so longingly for so many hours. I showed him apartments for rent in Fuentecastillo and also in the towns which had allotments nearby and he saw that, at least until the following summer, they were to be had for reasonable prices.

"And we'll get one cheaper than that after I've had a word," he said, "because there's hundreds of them empty all winter, I bet."

"We could go and visit the other towns and see which one we like best," I said.

"We could."

"It'll mean catching two buses, though," I added.

"Hmm, there's nowt wrong with Fuentecastillo as far as I can see."

"But your allotment, dear?"

"Aw, I don't need one of them. There'll be plenty of peace and quiet up along the beach and I'll be able to shoot up to my pal Pedro's allotment in half an hour when we get the car."

"A car!" I exclaimed with delight.

Ken stood up before I had chance to grab him, and lit his pipe.

"Pedro's getting a new one and he says he'll let me have the old one at a good price," he said through the smoke.

"And it's not like that old house?" I asked fearfully, having re-enacted the house proposal scene so many times in my mind.

"Five years old, regular services, not a scratch on it. It's a grand little car," he reassured me.

I must confess to the reader that after that wonderful conversation which changed my life from one of increasing despondency to one of renewed hope for the future I drank a total of five bottles of beer – to Ken's eight – which warmed up my feet wonderfully and sent me to bed in a rather tipsy, but very happy, state. The following day I bought the gas heater which Ken said should be ample for the coast and stop us freezing to death while we remained in the village, and after installing the spare bottle it did indeed enable us to watch Inspector Morse without all the annoying whirring of the fan heater.

"We'll leave all the gas bottles nice and empty for them southern sods," Ken said that evening over dinner.

"But what about the rent though, dear?" I asked. "I think we're supposed to pay it all even if we leave early."

"Oh, I'll pay them all right."

"Yes?" I said with surprise.

"In the next life," he concluded, before laughing demoniacally and leaving for the bar.

10

The next morning I was all for us catching the first bus down to Fuentecastillo to go apartment hunting, but Ken said that four bus trips in two days was too much for him and that we could go the following day. As soon as the sound of the moped died away as he puttered off to our good friend Pedro's allotment, I opened the computer and did not spare the dongle until I had made notes on every single apartment in Fuentecastillo which might meet our requirements. I saw that for just €100 more a month than the cheapest ones we would get a two bedroom one with air conditioning, telly satellite, and furniture and decor which looked very nice indeed, so I threw away the notes on the cheaper ones because we weren't *that* poor anyway.

I won't bore the reader with an account of the longest afternoon and evening of my life as I watched the clock tick away until bedtime. We watched another episode of Inspector Morse and I truly hoped that before the DVDs were finished we would have come down from the mountain and be settling into our new abode, hopefully before Christmas which was a mere three weeks away. On reflection, I said to Ken that I supposed we should stay, or at least pay, until the end of the month really, but he said we would leave when we damn well liked and would pay the rent up until the day we left, and leave fifty, or perhaps a hundred, euros for them for the bills.

On asking him why he was taking such an unforgiving approach to our landlords when he had always done everything 'by the book' in the past he said it was because of the empty gas bottles.

"Take us for northern noggins, do they?" he said. "After this they won't go near another northerner for the rest of their lives and we'll all be better off for it," he added with a cackle. "I'll leave the keys with Pedro and when they see that the rent money's not going into the bank they've have bloody kittens, the tight sods."

Although I didn't really approve of this way of going about things I dared not contradict my husband for fear of altering his new pro-coast feelings, and if that sounds like an excuse I must point out that none of you know Ken as well as I do, although I hope that by my truthful portrayal of him you are starting to get some idea of how his mind works. He now seemed as keen as I did to settle beside the sea and I was determined that no obstacles were to be put in his way until the lease was signed.

Our bus ride to Fuentecastillo that Friday morning can only have reinforced the tug of the sea on my husband as we drove out of a clinging wet village mist into splendid sunshine as we approached the coast. Ken had decided that the best thing to do would be to take a walk around the streets near the beach and look for 'se alquila' (to rent) signs on apartments that had a sea view. He also said that the higher up they were, the better, as there'd be less traffic noise and a better view, which made sense. He set off at a furious pace leaving a trail of pipe smoke behind him and when he spotted a promising apartment he made sure that the sea view was a good one – the first row of apartments, alas, were beyond our means – by striding about in the middle of the street, regardless of the tooting traffic, until he had lined up the apartment windows with the sea. He then asked me to note down the telephone number and mark the place on our street map.

After about an hour I had noted down eight promising apartments and we repaired to our usual bar for coffee. As I drank my café con leche I looked longingly at my notepad and wished that I had pleaded with Ken more effectively for permission to buy a mobile phone, because as things stood I saw that we would have to ring the numbers from the house due to Ken's distaste for public telephone, which he considers unclean.

His unseasonably early bottle of beer, however, seemed to galvanise him and I soon saw that he too was eyeing the notepad wistfully. Seeing my opportunity, I said that it was a pity that we would have to wait until we got home to ring about the apartments as it would be nice to view one or two while we were here and after a moment's silent meditation he drained his bottle and called the waiter.

"Vicente," he said, for they were already on first name terms on only our third visit. "Una cerveza y... hay telefono aquí?" (Is there a phone here?)

"Sí, Ken, está dentro," he replied. (Yes, Ken, it is inside.)

(It feels strange to write in Spanish, but I suppose I'll get used to it if I ever speak it as well as Ken does.)

After Ken had drained his bottle he led the way inside and rang the number of the apartment we had liked the best from outside. Here his Spanish did fail him a little and after opening the conversation with a confident 'Hola' he lapsed into English and told the person at the other end that he wished to see the apartment. On hanging up he told me that the man had said that he would come to meet us as soon as he was free, which proved to be about four minutes after we had returned to our table, so, as Ken said, they must be keen, and perhaps susceptible to a little friendly haggling.

We all walked round to the apartment and after we had glided up in the lovely smooth lift to the fifth (of six) floors and the young Spanish estate agent had opened the door, imagine my surprise when I found that it was the very apartment whose photos I had liked the best on the computer! The sunshine through the big windows gave the place a very summery feel and the apartment was furnished tastefully down to the last detail, including a balcony table and two chairs, one of which Ken sat down on to measure the view, which he reckoned was of about a third of the sea.

There was no such view from what would be our bedroom, but the smaller bedroom gave onto the balcony and Ken said later that he would have that single bed dismantled in a jiffy and buy a nice armchair from which to view the sea in winter, killing two birds with one stone, he said, as then we wouldn't have a spare room for intruders. This, as I said, he said later, but first came the skilful negotiating skills which he put into practice in order to beat down the price.

"How much then, mate," he said.

"€500 a month if you stay until the end of June, plus €500 deposit," said the dapper young man.

"€500 a month all year round or €400 until the end of June," said Ken.

"Impossible," said the man with a shake of the head.

"Take it," said Ken, drawing his wallet out of his trouser pocket, "or leave it," he concluded after slapping down a pile of notes the like of which I hadn't seen since he flummoxed the conservatory salesman into dropping the price so much that he ended up getting the sack (but we got our conservatory).

"Impossible," the man said again, but less haughtily.

"Six months down," Ken said as he counted out the €50 notes, "for all year round," he went on, mesmerising the man with the notes and his clever rhyme, "plus the deposit... makes €3500. Do you still say no way, José?"

"I'm Miguel. I have to ask boss," he said, having lost his calm and his good English.

"Ring this number tonight between seven and... five past and you've got a deal."

"We see."

"And we'll be moving in on Monday."

"We see. I go to office now."

"Adios, matey," Ken concluded with a gangster-like grin after scooping up the money and leading me out of the door.

On the trip back into the inhospitable mountains I asked Ken if he thought they would ring and if we shouldn't really have viewed some more apartments just in case.

"That one'll do us," he said, "and if they don't ring you can buy yourself one of them mobile phones."

"So you're that sure?" I asked.

"Didn't you see the chump's face? That apartment would stay empty all winter if it wasn't for us."

"And why were you carrying so much money?"

"It's always handy to have a bit of spare cash on you," he said smugly, because he always gets very smug when he's got a good deal. I worried then that he'd lose Pedro's friendship by haggling to the death about the car, but I can tell you now that that didn't happen as by the following afternoon we were driving around in it – that's why he'd had all that cash ready, he later confessed – and that same evening the estate agent *did* ring, and on the Monday we *did* move into the new apartment where I am writing these words now.

You can tell, I think, that I've made this little book as truthful and lively as I could, because it's funny that when everything starts to go right there doesn't seem to be so much to write about. Ken says that that's the time when these other writers start making folk do weird things and generally start making things up and that, in any case, the shorter the book, the less time people will have to waste reading it.

It's March now and starting to get warmer, but it's been wonderful spending the winter in the new apartment where we only had to turn on the gas heater in the evenings for a bit, unlike in the village where Shirley tells me that her wood burning stove must've got through two or three trees already. She comes down for a free lunch now and again – always in the apartment, of course, and always on a day when Ken has shot off to Pedro's allotment – and she's still trying to sell her poky house in that godforsaken village, poor thing.

Hella came down to see us too. She rang us first to see if we needed her to do any more 'work' for us, which I said we didn't, but she invited herself down anyway. She's keener than ever to move here now after she's seen our apartment and she says she's looking forward to getting to grips with the local men, which didn't shock me at all, Hella being Hella. *And* – as I said, it's all been good news since we moved here – who should we see one day, but Juan from the village working in one of the seafront restaurants! His cousin had got him the job and he's living with him and very happy to have finally moved out of the family home where he was starting to think he would be ending his days. Ken says we must be bloody magnets because most of the people we knew in the village will end up living here in the end, and even Pedro, who comes down and goes fishing with Ken some Sundays, says that now property's cheap he might get himself a weekend place.

I see a bit more of Ken now that we're down here too, as he only goes up to the allotment about twice a week and to his new 'local' three or four times. After trudging round for a few nights he finally settled on a rough and ready sort of place quite a way in from the sea where he says he's just about the only non-local there, which he's pleased with because most of them can't stand the 'bloody guiris'. (Ken's words, of course.)

I've made a few friends too, mainly British and Irish women who I started meeting in my favourite café and who all seem to have the same interests as me. We're all off on a trip to Gibraltar next week and I've been told to take a great big suitcase with me to be able to bring back lots of 'goodies', which I think means booze, tobacco and English food. I asked Ken and he says to bring it back nice and full, so he's certainly become more generous since we've been down here, even buying me a mobile phone for Christmas so I can call my local friends.

The only blip so far has been a short visit by Ken's mother two weeks ago. He grumbled and grunted about putting the single bed back together and it seemed like a long week having her around the place, but like Ken said, I won't have to cook sprouts again now till next year, God willing. Other than that it's been plain sailing and we're both looking forward to the spring and summer when Ken says they won't be so many tourists what with the state of the economy and everything and that, anyway, midsummer will be the time to go back and turf out the teacher and her 'partner' and sell the house so that we can buy an apartment here.

So that's the end of my story so far and the way things are at the moment, so nice and blissful, I doubt I'll have much to write about in the future, unless I start making things up, which is not my way. So 'Settling in Spain' is what we are most certainly doing and as for 'between the mountains and the sea', I know which I like best, and so does my Ken.

CPSIA information can be obtained at www.ICGtesting.com
Printed in the USA
LVOW10s1944230915

455415LV00028B/1697/P